DID NOT START

Misadventures in Running, Cycling and Swimming
(Book Three in the DNF Series)

George Mahood

Copyright © 2021 by George Mahood

All rights reserved. This book or any portion thereof may not be reproduced or used in any manner whatsoever without the express written permission of the author except for the use of brief quotations in a book review.

This edition published 2021 by George Mahood.

www.facebook.com/georgemahood
www.instagram.com/georgemahood
www.twitter.com/georgemahood
www.georgemahood.com

ONE

'I think I've done something really stupid,' said my wife, Rachel.

'What?'

'I've signed up for the Dartmoor Classic.'

'That's not stupid. That's brilliant news. I've been encouraging you to sign up for ages.'

'Yeah...'

'You'll be fine. It's only 68 miles. You've cycled 56 miles before and then ran a half marathon afterwards.'

'Er, that's why I think I've done something stupid.'

'What do you mean?'

'I didn't sign up for the 68 mile one. I've signed up for the 110 mile one like you.'

'Oh... wow,' I gulped. 'Even better!'

'The shorter one had sold out, but there were still a couple of spaces available on the big one. So I just clicked Enter. Will I die?'

'No, of course you won't die. I'm sure you'll love it.'

'You obviously don't have to cycle it with me.'

'I would love to cycle with you. It will be fun.'

'No, it won't be fun. I'll be far too slow for you.'

The Dartmoor Classic is a cycling sportive through and around the challenging terrain of Dartmoor National Park. Our super fit Spanish friends – Daniel and Marta – had both signed up for the Grande route too, but Daniel pulled out at the last minute because of some lame excuse that I can't remember.

'I would rather cycle with you than on my own,' I said.

'You will cycle with Marta, won't you?'

'I doubt she will want to cycle with me. The Dartmoor Classic will feel like a gentle little Sunday spin for her.'

Marta once finished first female in a 24-hour mountain bike race in the Pyrenees, so was in a completely different league to Rachel and me. But when we told Marta that Rachel had signed up too, she was adamant that we were all going to cycle together the entire way. This cranked Rachel's anxiety levels up another notch.

It was an early start on the morning of the event. We picked up Marta from her house at 4.30am and drove to the race HQ at Newton Abbot Racecourse. The riders of the two shorter distances – the Medio and Piccolo – had later start times than our Grande ride, so registration was quiet and easy.

'Honestly, please don't wait for me,' said Rachel as we gathered in the starting pen. 'I'll just plod around at my own speed. I'll see you at the finish.'

'Noooo,' said Marta. 'We all cycle together. It izza just

Did Not Start

a bit of fun. We are not racing.'

'Marta's right,' I said. 'It will be much more fun if we all cycle together.'

Rachel gave a shrug of acceptance, and we all set off together shortly after 6am pedalling through the suburbs of Kingsteignton. As with my previous experience of tackling the shorter distance of the Dartmoor Classic, the manageable pace of the other riders fooled me once again, forgetting that their speed was being dictated by the safety car up ahead. After a couple of miles, the car pulled over to the roadside and within seconds, most of the other riders disappeared into the distance, leaving us in their dust. Groups of cyclists started in waves about ten minutes apart, so we enjoyed a brief respite before being caught and overtaken by the later waves.

Shortly after passing through Bovey Tracey, we met the beast of Beckaford Hill. Beckaford Hill is a very steep and narrow road up onto the moor and is the only section of closed road on the entire course. During the Dartmoor Classic, cyclists using a GPS device and the Strava app can compare their times up this section against other riders. The fastest time of the day wins a special cycling kit and the honour of being the *King of the Mountains*.

Having tried to race up this hill during my previous Dartmoor Classic two years previously, I was curious to see how much (if at all) my fitness had improved.

As soon as we passed the *START* banner, I began to push a little harder.

'I'll see you at the top,' I said to Rachel and Marta, neither of whom had any desire to race.

I passed a few cyclists on my left who were taking it easy, and many faster ones came by me on my right. The road is very narrow and it's a bit of a challenge to stay out of people's way.

My lungs were burning like never before, my heart rate off the scale, and my legs were crying out in agony, but I was soon round the last bend and the cusp of the hill was in sight. As the road eventually levelled out at the top, I freewheeled to the side of the road, unclipped from my pedals and fell into a crumpled heap on the grass verge. I was in too much pain to pay any attention to the incredible views that I knew were sweeping below me.

It was a couple of minutes before Rachel and Marta appeared and I had still not managed to get my breathing under control. They had both taken their time, chatted to each other the whole way up, and Marta was not in the slightest bit out of breath. I climbed back on my bike and tagged along behind.

'Well done,' panted Rachel. 'You shot off up that hill like a bullet.'

'It... was... a... stupid... idea.' I gasped. 'I... I... feel... horrendous.'

But my regret intensified moments later when the Strava *FINISH* banner came into view a few hundred metres further on. Rather than have the finish line at the top of the hill, the official finish of the climb was further

Did Not Start

up the road, presumably so that everyone didn't stop like me and potentially block the top of the hill.

Most other riders apparently knew this as the roadside beyond the banner was littered with collapsed cyclists all trying to recover from their efforts. I crossed the line behind Rachel and Marta, meaning they were officially faster than me up Beckaford Hill.

Rachel's longest bike ride had been the 56-mile bike leg of the Cotswold triathlon a few weeks previously. That had almost all been on flat roads. Earlier in the year we had cycled 38 miles along the Exe Estuary to celebrate her 38th birthday. That had been pancake flat the entire way. She had done a few shorter rides around the hilly South Devon countryside where we live, but nothing over 25 miles. To put this into context, and bore you with some stats, the bike leg of the Cotswold 113 was 56 miles and had 991 feet of climbing. The Dartmoor Classic was 110 miles and had almost 10,000 feet of ascent, making it not only twice the distance, but proportionally five times as hilly. The Dartmoor Classic Grande was a big step up for me (and the toughest bike ride I had ever attempted), but a giant leap for Rachel.

For the first few long climbs, Marta and I cycled alongside Rachel, trying to offer words of encouragement and making small talk to try and provide a distraction for Rachel. It soon became clear that this wasn't appreciated. Rachel, understandably, found it demoralising having us talking to each other next to her when she was struggling to breathe.

So, on some steeper hills, Marta and I each cycled up at our own pace. Marta would then pull over at the top and wait for me, and the two of us would then wait for Rachel to catch us up. This seemed to incense Rachel even more, as she then felt like she was holding us back. And, unlike Marta and me, Rachel didn't have time to stop for a break at the top of each hill.

Despite living in Devon for four years and holidaying in the county all my life, it was only in the last year that we had started to spend any time on Dartmoor as a family. My cycle training for the Ironman had introduced me to the moor, and subsequent bike rides and family days-out had made it a familiar playground – largely thanks to letterboxing. I had still only seen a tiny fraction of the National Park, but each time I passed through, it inspired me to spend more and more time there. *I wonder where that track goes? That river looks like a good swim spot. I bet the kids would love to climb that tor.*

Unfortunately, on this occasion my enthusiasm was not shared by Rachel. At the summit of one of the long climbs about 30 miles in, she lost her shit completely. She became quite angry and emotional and insisted that Marta and I should push on ahead without her and that she would much prefer to cycle on her own. She also suggested that there was a very good chance she would pull out of the event completely as she was finding it so tough and unable

Did Not Start

to find any enjoyment from it at all.

'Just treat it as a day out on the bike,' I said.

'But it's not just a day out on the bike, George, IS IT? It's a bloody hard and hilly 110 miles!'

'Yes, it's a bloody hard and hilly day out on the bike, but that's all that it is. It doesn't matter how long it takes us.'

'But we are not even a THIRD of the way. There's NO WAY I am going to be able to complete it. It's only going to get worse from here. I might as well give up now.'

'You're doing great. You will complete it.'

'Please stop it, George. I know you're trying to help, but I honestly want you and Marta to carry on ahead without me.'

Marta was a little further up the road and had not heard our conversation, so I caught up with her to discuss what we should do. We faced a difficult dilemma. Marta and I were both really enjoying cycling with Rachel. But it was very clear that the feeling was not reciprocated. If we continued on without her and then she ended up pulling out, we would feel terribly guilty for not staying with her. But maybe Rachel would genuinely be happier without us?

'Of course we stay!' said Marta categorically. 'It iz much more fun with all of uz together.'

'That's what I think. But I don't think it's fun for Rachel.'

'She will be fine. She iz probably just hungry.'

Marta and I kept a little distance between us and Rachel

up the long hill towards Princetown, where there was a brief respite as we freewheeled down past Dartmoor Prison and into the day's first feed station.

Marta was right about the hunger, because reaching the Princetown feed station after 34 miles was a turning point in Rachel's mood. As well as the food, it was a chance for us all to get off our bikes, stretch our legs and take a much-needed break from pedalling.

The feed station on the Dartmoor Classic is legendary and was pretty much the only reason I signed up for the event again. It's definitely the only reason I signed up for the Grande route, as you get to visit it twice.

Rather than the standard fare of energy gels and bruised bananas, the feed stations are plentiful banquets of sandwiches, crisps, cakes, biscuits and homity pie. We each filled a plate and sat on the grass to eat our picnics.

Shortly after the feed station, Rachel would have a decision to make. Cyclists reach a junction where the Grande riders turn right towards Tavistock, completing a huge loop of about 40 miles before returning for their second visit to the feed station at Princetown. Those doing the shorter Medio route turn left onto the more direct route back towards the finish in Newton Abbot. This was the only possible get-out clause for riders wanting to shorten their route.

'How are you fweeling?' I asked Rachel, as I stuffed my face with a cheese sandwich filled with added crisps.

'Better. Thanks. Sorry for being so grumpy.'

Did Not Start

'Don't apologise. I'm finding it really tough too.'

'I just wasn't expecting it to be this tough.'

'What's your plan? Are you going to keep going and do the long route?'

'I don't know. What do you think?'

'I think you should definitely do the longer route. You'll only regret it if you don't.'

'But I just feel like I'm holding you and Marta up.'

'Stop saying zat!' said Marta bluntly. 'I like not racing. I LOVE not racing.'

'Ok, if you are sure.'

'We are sure.'

We reached the junction and I glanced at Rachel to double-check she was still planning on turning right. I stuck out my right arm and she did the same.

This was all unchartered territory for me. On my previous Dartmoor Classic, I had cycled the Medio route and turned left, shaking my head in disbelief that anyone would sign up to the longer route and feeling extremely grateful that I wasn't as foolish as those deranged cyclists. And now here I was, one of those deranged cyclists.

The next few miles lulled us into a false sense of ease, as we came down off the moor following long sweeping bend after bend. Rachel's mood had changed completely. I wouldn't go as far as saying she was enjoying herself, but a switch had been flicked and she was at least acceptant of her situation. Unlike with some other events that we had taken part in, signing up to the Grande route had been all

Rachel's doing. It was like she suddenly realised that it had been her stupid idea, and so she had to just suck it up and make the most of it. On this occasion, she could not blame me.

The fact that we needed to do very little pedalling for several miles definitely had something to do with her mood change. I didn't have the heart to tell Rachel that we were eventually going to have to cycle back up to Princetown and that every metre we descended would be another metre we had to climb later in the day. It had been a cold start to the morning, but it had warmed up considerably and it was a magnificent day to be out on the moor.

We passed through the villages of Walkhampton and Horrabridge, descending further and further until we reached the pretty town of Tavistock. I had hoped this would mark the point at which we would begin to turn back east towards Princetown, but we passed straight through the town centre and continued west up a long climb out of town in the opposite direction to the finish. Thankfully, Rachel's sense of direction is appalling, so it didn't make any difference to her.

Marta and I cycled up each hill at our own pace and then made sure Rachel was ready to continue before we set off again. There were faint glimmers of enjoyment, interspersed with moments of rage and frustration (a bit like life in general), as we climbed up and down through Chillaton and then did a loop that dropped down steeply into Lydford Gorge – the deepest in the South West –

before passing the familiar sights of Brentor Church perched high on its prominent peak. This is the church I had bored my friends Simon and Ross about during our Dartmoor Way bike ride a couple of months previously. I tried my luck with Rachel and Marta.

'That's Brentor Church up on that hill.'

No response.

'Legend has it that some sea merchant in days of yore (whatever that means) was caught in a tremendous storm created by the devil. The merchant pleaded with god to be saved and when his ship miraculously made it to dry land, he devoted his life to god and committed to building a church on the highest point he could see. And that was Brentor. But then every night when they tried to build the church, the devil knocked it down and they had to start again.'

'Hmm, that's interesting,' panted Rachel, but I couldn't tell if she was being serious or mocking me.

'Fascinating,' said Marta, her Spanish accent not being enough to hide the sarcasm.

The hills between Tavistock and Princetown were probably the toughest of the day. With 70 miles already in our legs, the road climbed for several miles back up onto the open moor. And when we reached the top of the longest hill just below the imposing peak of Cox Tor, the road descended cruelly into the hamlet of Merrivale, before crossing the river Walkham and climbing once again up the other side of the valley. It was fairly demoralising, but the views were stunning, and Dartmoor certainly took our breath away, in a quite literal way.

I pulled over to the side of the road at the top of one of the long drags before Princetown and a Dartmoor pony wandered over to me. It seemed particularly friendly and was nuzzling up to me inquisitively. I then realised it was trying to get into my bike bag and steal one of my energy gels. I had to wrestle one from its teeth. Feeding Dartmoor ponies is a criminal offence, and I thought that would go down as a pretty spectacular DNF to be disqualified from the race and then charged with unwittingly feeding a pony an energy gel. Although, a Dartmoor pony jacked up on sugar and caffeine would have been a highly entertaining sight.

Rachel was in good spirits by the time we reached the feed station at Princetown for the second time. Now that the hardest two-thirds of the race were behind us, she really did look like she was enjoying herself. We filled another plate of food each and, as we were eating, I spotted a familiar figure standing by the bike racks. Vanessa was the mum of a friend of ours. She was in her mid-60s and had taken up sport (and specifically triathlon) in her late 50s. She enjoyed it so much that she progressed up to Ironman distance and now represents Great Britain in the 65+ category.

Rachel and I chatted briefly to Vanessa and then

introduced her to Marta. Vanessa then said goodbye, climbed on her bike and we waved her off as we continued to eat our sandwiches and cake.

'What are we doing?' said Marta when Vanessa was out of sight.

'What do you mean?' I said.

'We can't let that old lady beat us!'

Rachel and I laughed. Marta was smiling too, but there was also something deadly serious about her tone.

'She's not an old lady. She's a GB athlete.'

'Yes, but she iz still old. There iz no excuse to let 'er beat us.'

I laughed again, but Marta's eyes remained steely cold.

'Are you serious?'

'Of course! Come on, VAMOS! We go... NOW!'

Marta had spent 70 miles happily cycling along at a steady pace with no desire to push, but now beating the old lady was suddenly the most important thing in the world.

I looked at Rachel, who was quietly devouring a chocolate brownie.

'Alright, fine, I'm coming,' she said.

We pushed hard for the next few miles and eventually caught sight of Vanessa ahead. We said hello as we passed, and she didn't seem to make any effort to try and keep up with us. On the next hill, Marta and I pulled ahead from Rachel slightly, but when we waited for her at the top, Vanessa reached us before Rachel and passed without stopping and began descending the hill on the other side.

'Zee old lady is ahead of uz again!' cursed Marta. 'Where iz Rachel?'

'She'll be here soon. You go ahead if you're so keen to beat her.'

'No, no, I'm only joking,' she said.

But she wasn't joking.

Rachel reached the top a minute later and pulled over to the side of the road to rest.

'NO TIME TO STOP!' shouted Marta. 'Zee old lady is ahead of uz! VAMOS!'

'Please,' begged Rachel, 'Just give me a minute... I can't breathe.'

Marta smiled to try and hide the fact that she was raging inside.

We made good progress over the next few miles and caught and overtook Vanessa once again just before the town of Moretonhamstead.

'Right, we must not let 'er overtake uz again,' said Marta.

'I'll try,' said Rachel. 'How far is it to the finish?'

'Only about 16 miles,' I said. 'And most of that is downhill. There is one big hill coming up, though.'

I remembered the long, slow drag out of Moretonhamstead from my previous Dartmoor Classic. It's not especially steep, but it goes on a long way. And as it comes after 90 miles of cycling, it is pretty tough on the legs.

Marta and I got into a bit of a rhythm and soon reached

Did Not Start

the top, where we pulled over to the side of the road to wait for Rachel.

'I really 'ope Rachel makes it up zee 'ill ahead of zee old lady,' said Marta.

'I'm sure she will.'

'Because if it iz downhill from 'ere to the finish, we might not be able to catch 'er.'

'Don't worry about it. We will beat her.'

Racing had not even been a consideration to me before the second feed station, but now part of me had also taken on Marta's desire to beat the old lady. I mean Vanessa. It was quite exciting to have an extra challenge within a challenge. Even though Vanessa wasn't aware we were racing against her. A few minutes later, a familiar figure came into view over the crest of the hill. But it wasn't Rachel. It was the old lady. I mean Vanessa.

'NOOO!' shouted Marta. 'She iz going to beat uz. What are we going to do? Where iz Rachel?'

Marta was looking frantic, half laughing, half seething.

I had a plan.

'Vanessa!' I called out. 'How are you doing? How did you find that hill? Did you see Rachel?'

I fired off a few questions so that she would have to slow down. My plan worked better than expected as she pulled over to join us at the side of the road.

'I think I passed Rachel a little further down the hill. She looked like she was struggling a bit.'

'Would you like a crisp?' I said, offering her one from

the pack I had just opened.

'Oh, ok, thanks,' she said.

Just then, Marta and I caught sight of Rachel crawling slowly over the brow of the hill. Crawling slowly on her bike, that is, not on all fours.

'Here, have them all,' I said, handing the entire packet to Vanessa and jumping on my bike.

Marta was already aboard hers and cycling slowly towards the top of the next descent.

'Well done, Rachel. It's all downhill from here,' I said.

'Wait... can I... I just need...'

'No time for that,' said Marta. 'VAMOS!'

'See you in a bit, Vanessa,' I said, as we left her standing on the roadside with my packet of crisps. I expected her to jump on her bike and race after us, but she just stood there looking a little bemused.

The final 15 miles are some of the easiest of the route. The road descends for several fast miles off the moor down into Kingsteignton before following relatively flat roads through residential streets to the finish at Newton Abbot Racecourse.

Every so often I would wind Marta up by telling her I could see the old lady (sorry, Vanessa) behind us, and each time she would fall for it and put on a burst of speed. Rachel had nothing left in her legs but was feeling absolutely elated by what she had achieved. We entered the grounds of Newton Abbot Racecourse, and all crossed the finish line together in a time of 9h 52m.

Did Not Start

Vanessa finished four minutes behind us, which delighted Marta immensely.

'We did it!' I said to Rachel.

'We did it,' she said.

'I'm so impressed. 110 miles! That's amazing.'

'Oh god, that was so tough. Sorry for being so awful for the first half.'

'It was really tough. You did so well to keep going. I'm sorry if we annoyed you. Are you glad we rode together?'

'Definitely. I'm not sure if I would have continued if I was on my own.'

We racked our bikes and went over to the building to collect our medals. As we approached the door, a woman in a high-vis jacket blocked our way.

'I'm sorry, the building is currently closed due to an explosion,' she said.

'An explosion? What happened?'

'We think a gas burner caught fire. It should all be sorted soon.'

We could see smoke coming from a vent at the side of the building and within a few minutes two fire engines arrived at the scene. We sat in the racecourse's grandstand and rested our legs, wondering whether to wait around or just go home.

'I would quite like my medal,' said Rachel.

'Me too,' I said.

Marta was not allowed to admit she wanted a medal for finishing almost last in a cycling sportive. It wasn't the Spanish way. But we could tell she wanted one too. 841 riders started the Grande route, and we finished 820th, but we were still as deserving of a medal as the riders who finished over four hours ahead of us.

After about 45 minutes, they declared the building safe, the emergency services dispersed, and they opened the doors for the remaining handful of cyclists to collect their medals. We went up to a desk and the race official typed Rachel's bib number into the computer. They printed her a ticket with her finishing time and splits and gave her a medal. The same happened for Marta.

When they entered my bib number into the computer, a puzzled look spread across the lady's face.

'Hmmm, it has got you down as Did Not Start.'

'Did not START? What?'

'According to the computer system, you didn't pass any of the timing checkpoints or the finish line. It says you didn't even cross the start line.'

Rachel and Marta gave a snort of laughter.

'Oh, that's weird. I definitely did!' I said.

'Well, I can't print you off a finishing time, I'm afraid, as there isn't one. You are technically down as DNS.'

I was standing there in my cycling kit, looking tired and grubby. It's possible I could have faked it all in order to get a medal, but it was unlikely.

Did Not Start

'I tell you what, I can see that it looks like you did take part today so I can give you a medal, but as there is no record of you passing through the checkpoints, you won't appear on the official results.'

'Ok, that's fine, thank you. I can live with that. I did complete it, though, I promise. I can even show you a selfie that I took of me with one of the ponies up near Princetown, if you like.'

The lady stared at me blankly.

'Um, no, thanks. That won't be necessary.'

I checked the official results later and discovered that although we had crossed the finish line four minutes before the old lady, her start time had been eleven minutes after ours, so she had actually beaten us by seven minutes. I never told Marta.

TWO

As soon as our three children – Layla (aged 10), Leo (aged 8) and Kitty (aged 5) – broke up from school for the summer holidays, we drove to Croyde in North Devon to meet some friends for four night's camping. We had booked a site with spectacular sweeping views all along Croyde Bay. It must be one of the best locations for a campsite in the UK... if the weather is fine. When the weather is bad – as it was for our entire four days' stay – anywhere on earth would be better. With nothing between us and the wild Atlantic Ocean, we were fully exposed to the full force of mother nature for the whole holiday.

While many of the surrounding campers packed up their tents and headed home (some even deciding it was too wet for their campervans), we decided to stick it out. We were fortunate that the rain relented a little most evenings – the ferocious wind never leaving us – and we created a makeshift windbreak by parking all our cars tightly together in front of our tents. This hindered our sea views somewhat. Not wanting to be deterred, we stubbornly cooked outside each night, using our gas stoves

Did Not Start

and barbecues in the little shelter provided by our cars.

We have had wet and windy camping holidays before. But not like this. This was a different level of misery. Our last 'camping' trip as a family had been our two-night stay in a static caravan for the Cotswold 113 familiarisation weekend. It had given us a taste of how some other campers live, and Rachel's love of camping had taken a massive hit. It had been a precariously balanced relationship before Croyde, but each passing hour of the cold and grim weather convinced her more and more that sleeping in a tent in the UK is not all it is cracked up to be.

One of our friends had brought a small one-man tent and the weather was so bad we genuinely thought the wind would carry him away in the night. So he moved his tent inside the cavernous living area of our other friend's 8 berth family tent. The wind was so severe that the one-man tent continued to move and flap around all night, even when pitched inside another.

There's only so much time during daylight hours that you can spend trapped in a tent with young children, so we stayed outside as much as possible. We went on walks up and around the rugged headland of Baggy Point, played in the vast sand dunes behind Croyde beach, and Rachel and I each squeezed in a couple of blustery runs along the coast path during the holiday. Seeing as Croyde is one of the most popular surf spots in the UK, we took a couple of surfboards and several body boards with us and made the most of the perfect surfing conditions brought on by the horrendous weather. My friend Mark and I spent about two hours being well and truly humiliated by the sea. It was brilliant fun, but we each managed to stay upright for only a few seconds at best. Leo asked if he could have a go, so I talked him through what he needed to do, even though it clearly hadn't worked for me, and helped him get ready for a wave. I gave the board a gentle push and he jumped to his feet and rode the wave all the way to the shore.

'Is this right, Dad?' he said, looking back casually over his shoulder.

'Er... yep, that's pretty good. Well done!' I said.

Mark shook his head in disbelief.

'That's not fair,' he said.

'Must be beginners' luck,' I said.

'Can I have another go?' said Leo, wading towards me with the board.

'Of course. You made that look so easy. See if you can do it again.'

The next wave was slightly bigger, and I helped set him off. He jumped to his feet and again surfed it all the way to shore. He looked back and I gave him a big thumbs up, while cursing under my breath.

'That's so annoying,' I said. 'We've been doing this for two hours.'

'I know. It must his size and the low centre of gravity or something,' said Mark.

'Yeah, it must be. It can't be anything to do with our shitness.'

Did Not Start

'Definitely not.'

'Want another go?' I called to Leo.

'No thanks,' he said with a '*what's all the fuss about? It's easy!*' tone. 'I'm done now. Thanks, it was fun.'

There were plenty of positives to take away from the holiday. It is amazing how cold and wet weather can give you a new level of appreciation for life's comforts. That first cup of hot tea each morning, drunk from a tin cup and made with water boiled on a gas stove, tasted like an elixir. I then walked in the wind and rain to the small shop in a nearby holiday park and bought croissants and pain au chocolate for everyone. It may have been the situation, or the accompaniment of a nice cafetière of coffee back in the tent, but the pastries almost made the suffering worth it. I have eaten a lot of pain au chocolates in my time – including all over France – but none of them were as good as those from a North Devon holiday park.

On one particularly wet day, we all drove to Ilfracombe and went to the cinema. I can't even remember what the film was, but it was a special kind of paradise sitting on comfy seats in the warm and dry for two hours, again allowing us a new appreciation for things we take for granted.

On the final evening, a severe weather warning was issued – as if it hadn't been severe enough already. We didn't want to pack up all our wet things and go home early, but we also didn't want to wait around in our tents if the weather was going to be as bad – and potentially dangerous – as predicted. We pegged our tents down a little tighter, parked our cars in their windbreak formation, and then spent the evening in the restaurant-bar of the neighbouring holiday park. Big burgers, greasy fries, cold beer and a soft play area to keep the kids amused. It was honestly one of the best evenings of my life.

We woke on the morning of our final day to full sunshine, and by late morning our tents were completely dry. Despite the weather, it had been a fun and character-building few days.

A few weeks later, we headed off on another family holiday to try and help Rachel recover from the trauma of our Croyde camping trip. Unfortunately, this too was in a tent. But thankfully, this one was in France.

We spent two weeks without a drop of rain, enjoying lots of incredible French food and wine, swimming in the sea at our first campsite and a slow meandering river at our second. Rachel's enthusiasm for camping had been reignited.

Both of our campsites were adjacent to one of the thousands of dedicated cycle paths that stretch the length and breadth of France. In between these cycle paths are miles and miles of quiet minor roads. And the roads in France are incomparable to those in Britain. They are all immaculately surfaced – even tiny rural roads in the middle of nowhere – and it is very rare to see a pothole out in the countryside. France has a very similarly sized population to the UK but spread out over a country more than twice as big, and with a road network twice its length, so it is no wonder they all feel so quiet.

With these endless opportunities to explore the French countryside, Rachel and I were eager to do as much cycling as possible. Like last year, there had not been room to bring my bike to France, so we took it in turns to head out on hers. It was the perfect place for the children to cycle, too. But despite her enjoyment of the pump track at Haldon Forest earlier in the year, our youngest daughter Kitty (now almost six) continued to have a turbulent relationship with her bike. She viewed it as the transport of the devil and was hugely reticent each time we brought up the idea of a family bike ride. With an absence of jumps or obstacles to keep her enthused, we had to try to improve the negative connotations associated with family bike rides. Rather than going out cycling, we would head out for ice-creams or churros... on our bikes. It was an attempt to try to rebrand cycling to Kitty, and make it all about the destination, rather than the journey. It usually worked for the first half of each bike ride, but the return trip – once the bribe had been used up – was always a lot more tedious. With Rachel's low tolerance for the stop/start nature of cycling with young children, she usually opted to run while I cycled with the kids, and then on the return journey when Kitty was at her most stubborn, Rachel would run off ahead, back to the campsite with Leo and Layla, while I acted as

Kitty's exasperated sweeper vehicle.

In towns and villages all over France (and most of Europe), the bicycle seems to have secured itself as a more viable means of transport than it has in the UK. You'll see people of all ages out riding bikes, and most of them are dressed as they would be for the rest of their day. There will be men in suits, women in trousers or long flowing dresses, and very few of them will have made any effort to dress specifically for cycling. A more reliable and temperate climate obviously helps, but it was refreshing to see this more relaxed attitude to cycling. A common obstacle that prevents people from exercising is that they claim they don't have the correct kit. There is far too much obsession with attire, and most of it is unnecessary.

I have friends who have put off running for years because they didn't own any dedicated running kit. You don't need a dedicated running kit. Be like the French and wear whatever you feel comfortable in. A pair of trainers are important, but that doesn't mean they have to be expensive. I've been for a proper running shoe fitting only once in my life and ended up with a pair of trainers that caused no end of pains and problems. Since then, I have always had an aversion to buying dedicated running kit.

I tend to wear my trainers until my feet literally fall out of the bottom. Even then I'm reluctant to throw them away and have built up a sizable collection of old trainers that might (definitely won't) come in handy one day.

Did Not Start

I wear a cheap pair of shorts and any old t-shirt (usually one of many event souvenir t-shirts that I've acquired over the years). I do wear a GPS watch, but only because I like to keep track of my runs, not because I need to. I usually carry my phone in an elasticated running belt for listening to podcasts, taking photos or in case of an emergency, but find running equally enjoyable – and often more so – when I leave it at home.

Rachel has a habit of forgetting our wedding anniversary. At the time of writing this book, we have been married for 16 years. She has forgotten our anniversary for about half of those. The other eight years, she has only remembered at the last minute after being reminded by her mum or sister.

This year, shortly before our summer holiday, we celebrated our 13th anniversary. The traditional gift for 13 years is lace, which opened up lots of possibilities for a provocative anniversary gift.

Instead, I bought her some elastic 'no tie' shoelaces for her trainers. Now that she was a triathlete, saving those precious seconds while tying and untying laces in transition was surely important. Well, not crucial enough for me to have my own set of elastic laces, or for Rachel to ever get around to threading hers into her trainers, but it saved me an uncomfortable *Father Ted* style visit to the lingerie department.

You don't need elastic shoelaces in your trainers. They

won't make you a better runner.

Another common reason that prevents people heading out to exercise in public is feeling self-conscious about what others will think. This is also a misconception. Other runners and cyclists will be too absorbed by their own pain, suffering or perhaps euphoria to be in the least bit judgemental about what you look like or what you are wearing.

There is usually a welcome camaraderie amongst cyclists, runners and walkers. Almost all will acknowledge you as you pass each other, in a subtle but knowing way that recognises that you too have decided to head out your door and stretch your legs. It doesn't matter your age, weight or level of fitness; when you pass another person out exercising you already share a lot in common with them.

Midway through our second week in France, my mum and dad came to visit for a day. They were in the middle of their own cycling holiday in Brittany and called into our campsite. I borrowed my dad's bike for the afternoon and Rachel and I headed off together while my parents looked after the children. We cycled 32 miles on wonderfully smooth and wide roads, through the beautiful French countryside, interspersed with quaint little villages. We stopped for ice-cream and coffee halfway and looped back around to our campsite by late afternoon. It was the first time Rachel and I had cycled together in France and after

Did Not Start

hearing all about my mum and dad's own French cycle tour, it got me excited about possible multi-day cycling holidays in France at some point in the future.

THREE

Earlier in the year, I signed up to the Moor2Sea cycling sportive thinking it was going to be the year I became a proper cyclist. I knew I would have the Dartmoor Classic under my belt and assumed I would be raring to take on another. The race took place on the morning after getting home from France, and I arrived at the start at Exeter Racecourse feeling flustered, sleep deprived, and not looking forward to it in the slightest. There had been three distance options for the More2Sea: the 34-mile Inspire route, the 70-mile Challenge route, and the 112-mile Extreme route. Having taken on the longer route of the Dartmoor Classic, I felt like I could not then step down to a shorter ride so foolishly signed up for the Extreme.

Unlike the Dartmoor Classic with Rachel and Marta, nobody wanted to sign up for this one with me, so I was riding solo. I already missed their company and I had not even started pedalling.

Exeter Racecourse is located a few miles southwest of Exeter, sitting on top of Haldon Hill which towers over the surrounding countryside. This meant for an easy start to the race, as the only way was down. In fact, the first 25 miles were a delight, as the road descended from Haldon and then headed out towards the mouth of the River Exe at Dawlish, where we followed wide and level roads along the coast to Teignmouth. From Teignmouth we cycled parallel to the Teign Estuary, with fishing boats moored on the exposed mud flats. The road undulated slightly, but I felt like I was flying. For the first 20 miles, I had an average speed of over 20mph, which is completely unheard of for me. *Look at me go!* I thought to myself. *I AM a proper cyclist! I am a machine!* I was overtaking the occasional cyclist and not even out of breath. *Cycling is a piece of cake!*

And then we reached Dartmoor, and everything fell apart. We started climbing onto the moor on a route similar to sections of the Dartmoor Classic, and my speed rapidly plummeted into single figures and all those I had confidently overtaken, gradually passed me. I had allowed myself to get carried away by the kind roads and easy gradient, when I should have been pacing myself and not going into the red before reaching the first proper hill of the day.

Soon after leaving Bovey Tracey, the climb to Haytor began. The rocky outcrop of Haytor is one of Dartmoor's most popular spots. It is not an exceptionally steep ascent, but is long and unrelenting, continuing for over three miles with an average gradient of 6.4%. It is an iconic climb, with a stage of the Tour of Britain ending here in 2016 and the venue of the British National Hill Climb Championships in 2019.

There was an added incentive to push harder on this section. The sportive organisers were offering a special prize to those riders who reached the top of the Haytor climb inside a particular time. And this special prize? A tiny little pin badge. It's amazing what grown men and women will put themselves through just to get their hands on a badge.

Despite feeling wrecked from the start of the climb, I gave it a little extra and tried to get into a comfortable rhythm. For most of the climb, you get the demoralising sight of what is to come, with the road snaking way off up into the distance ahead. As I approached the top, with the dramatic granite rocks of Haytor over to my right, I glanced at my watch and tried to calculate how long it had taken me since the start of the hill. By my unreliable calculations, I hoped I was just inside the time limit to receive a pin badge.

If I had forfeited that pin badge for an easier ascent of Haytor, the rest of the day might have been more enjoyable. As it was, from then on, it just got worse and worse. Each hill brought on a whole new level of suffering, and I experienced a deepened sense of empathy with how Rachel must have felt during the Dartmoor Classic. I kept trying to search for positives, but they proved evasive.

There was the occasional pleasant moment, interspersed within the gloom. The route and the views were stunning, and although we cycled on many of the

Did Not Start

roads I had been on before, we also visited some parts of Dartmoor that were new to me. We passed through tiny villages, across stone bridges with children splashing around in the river below, slowing down to avoid ponies and sheep on the road. All the while I was making mental notes of places to come back to with the family, and trying to distance myself from how horrendous I was feeling.

The beautiful YHA Dartmoor Hostel in the remote location of Bellever near Postbridge – once a rare breeds farm – had been transformed into a feed station for the day and provided much needed relief. My body felt broken, and I had not even reached halfway. Shortly after the feed station, riders of the shorter route turned right back towards Haldon Hill while the Extreme riders turned left to do a big loop through Princetown, Yelverton, Ivybridge, Buckfastleigh and then back up onto the moor, returning to the YHA Dartmoor feed station for a second time. I paused at the junction for a couple of minutes, weighing up my options. Even if I took the shorter route, I would still have cycled 70 miles. That is still a bloody long way. I would be marked down as a DNF. But who would care?

I was just about to clip in and take the shorter route, when another rider approached the junction from behind. I had chatted with him briefly at the feed station.

'Turn left,' he said.

'I'm not sure I can do it.'

'You can. It's not as bad as you think it'll be. You'll be back at this junction before you know it. And then you can turn right next time.'

'Ha, ok, thanks.'

He turned left and continued up the road. I spent a few more seconds standing astride my bike at the junction, arguing internally with myself, then clipped in and reluctantly turned left. I knew it was going to be tough and I knew it was going to be unpleasant, but I also knew that the disappointment and regret I would have felt later if I turned right would have been worse.

I took a bit of extra care along the section of the B3212 between Postbridge and Two Bridges. Since the early 1900s, there have been a disproportionate number of accidents along this stretch of road – many of them with fatalities. What eerily links several of these crashes are reports of a pair of hairy hands emerging from nowhere, gripping the steering wheel, handlebars or reigns, and forcing the person from the road. The hairy hands do not discriminate against the mode of transport, as cars, pony and traps, cyclists, coach drivers, motorcyclists, lorry drivers and even some nearby campers have all fallen victim. Locals are quite dismissive of the legend and put it down to out-of-town 'grockles' not knowing how to drive on Devon roads. But over the years, some prominent, well-respected local citizens – including a doctor and an army captain – all shared the same stories of their encounters with the legend of Hairy Hands. The old bridge where the B3212 crosses Cherry Brook is now commonly known as

Did Not Start

Hairy Hands Bridge. Thankfully, the only thing gripping my handlebars during the Moor2Sea were my own hairy hands.

After about 62 miles, the route came down off the moor, which brought brief respite to the legs as we cycled on quick roads through the towns and villages of Ivybridge, Bittaford, South Brent and Buckfastleigh, before I remembered that the bastard route had to go all the way back up onto the moor again. The final third of the race, from about the 76-mile point, until the finish after 112 miles, was the most miserable I have ever felt on a bike. There were several points during those 36 miles that I was closer to quitting than I have ever been before. If it wasn't for the feed stations, then I definitely would.

Like the Dartmoor Classic, you are awarded a different medal depending on your finish time. I didn't care in the slightest about the colour of my medal. My only desire was for it all to be over. As I walked into the feed station at YHA Dartmoor for the second time, I chatted to a guy who was sitting with a plate full of food and a cup of tea.

'Good job these breaks don't count as part of your finishing time,' he said.

'Don't they?' I said. 'I thought it would be the total time for the whole ride, including all stops.'

'Nah, it's just the time you are actually on the course. You're allowed to stop at the feed stations for as long as you like.'

'Yeah, I know you're allowed to stop for as long as you

like, I just assumed that the clock wouldn't stop just because we did?'

'Well, good job it does. I'm going to fill up another plate and get another cuppa.'

I ate a couple of sandwiches, stuffed some cake into my mouth, downed a cup of sugary tea, burning off most of my tongue and throat in the process, thanked the volunteers, and bid farewell to the other cyclist who still had a large stack of cake to get through.

As I picked up my bike and headed back onto the road, I noticed there were no timing mats or scanners outside the feed station, so there would be no way for the organisers to factor in riders' stopping breaks. It was definitely the total elapsed time that was being recorded. Oh well, I didn't want to ruin his long, leisurely lunch break.

The route of the Dartmoor Classic had been more forgiving, with the final 20 miles by far the easiest of the day. The Moor2Sea is weighted heavily the other way, with a deceptively easy start and then cranking up the hills throughout the day, saving the worst until last.

If I'm feeling particularly tired or lazy during rides from home, I occasionally get off my bike and walk. There is no shame in walking. But I don't think I had ever got off my bike and walked during an event. It wasn't so much the embarrassment that had prevented me in the past; it was more the fact I would be admitting to myself that I was defeated. But on three or four separate occasions during those final 36 miles of the Moor2Sea, I was well and truly defeated. I got off my bike midway up each hill and walked. I had simply been trying to keep the pedals turning, not concerned about the speed at which I got up each hill, just wanting to make it to the top. But on each occasion, my legs just got to the point that they were moving so slowly that I was forced to unclip before toppling onto the road. On a couple of occasions, even the walking was too much of a challenge, and I sat down at the side of the road.

Some riders offered words of encouragement when they saw me collapsed at the roadside. Others kept their head low, in their own world of misery. A couple of others saw me sitting in the grass and could not resist the overwhelming temptation, so unclipped and collapsed on the verge next to me. We didn't speak to each other. No words were needed.

It was often impossible to get going again on such steep inclines. So I walked – my shoes clicking along the tarmac like clogs – until the gradient eased enough for me to remount.

Each time I stopped, I contemplated calling it a day. If the race finish had been somewhere more accessible – somewhere I could have turned and freewheeled to – then I'm certain I would have. But, unfortunately, the race finish – and more importantly, my car – was at the top of another fucking big hill.

I couldn't face the shame of calling the race support to ask to be driven the final few miles back to the finish to be officially marked as a DNF. If it came to it, I could always just take my cycling shoes off and walk my bike back up to the top of Haldon Hill in my socks. There would be no shame in that. Well, perhaps a little, but I was way past caring.

I knew if I called the race support, then hours later – when it was all over, and my body felt a little less wrecked – I would be mightily disappointed with myself for getting so far and effectively giving up. I was already annoyed with myself for pacing my race so badly and being defeated by each of those final hills.

From Moretonhamstead we climbed yet again, before a long descent off the moor. This time, far from enjoying the descent, I resented every metre, knowing that the further we descended, the further we would have to climb back up to the finish.

We followed a brief section of level road alongside a pleasant stream before the village of Doddicombsleigh (which sounds as though they couldn't agree on a name for the settlement so just squashed all the possibilities together). From here, the road climbed another 600ft back up to the finish at Exeter Racecourse.

With about a mile to go, on a particularly steep section where I was weaving all over the road, trying desperately to stay on my bike, I was overtaken by the man I had met in the Postbridge feed station who had been enjoying his extended picnic.

Did Not Start

'Alright chap?' he said. 'Nearly there.'

'Yeah, nearly there. I'll be so glad when this is over. Well done, buddy.'

As I crested the top of the hill, my emotions overcame me and I began to cry. But this wasn't a happy swell of positivity about what I had achieved. It was a feeling that I had been thoroughly beaten. Riding solo, there was no shared sense of accomplishment. Nobody I could laugh with about how horrendous it had been. Nobody I could swear 'never again' to and then sign up for next year's one a few days later.

As I walked into the race HQ to collect my medal, I heard the familiar voice of the cyclist who had passed me on the last hill. But he didn't sound so enthusiastic and positive this time.

'But I assumed the clock would stop for the feed stations?' he said curtly to the lady behind the desk.

'No, the clock keeps running, I'm afraid.'

'But if I had known that I would not have taken such a long break.'

'I'm sorry.'

'Look, here is my ride on my Strava. It shows my moving time as 7 hours 40 minutes, which is well inside the time to get a silver medal.'

'Yes, but it shows your elapsed time as being 8 hours and 30 minutes.'

'But that's because I thought the feed stations didn't

count.'

'I'm sorry. There's nothing we can do about it. We can't override the electronic timing system. Let me just check your Haytor climb on the system. Yes, you got your pin badge. Very well done.'

She handed him his bronze medal and pin badge.

'Thanks,' he said, sulkily turning away. He lifted his head and saw me.

'Apparently those feed station breaks DO get included in your time after all,' he said.

'Ah, that's annoying for you. Still, at least you made the most of all that cake.'

'That's true,' he smiled. 'It was bloody good cake.'

I had finished just inside the time limit for a bronze medal, and after an anxious pause, was also awarded my Haytor pin badge, which was a mild consolation for a truly testing day on the bike.

Did Not Start

FOUR

In November, Rachel and I took another trip to Pensilva for my fourth (and Rachel's second) Cornish Marathon. It was becoming a familiar event on the calendar. Another year, another Cornish Marathon, another hoodie (this time a weird Boy Scout green colour), another pasty and cup of tea, and another chance to meet Danny Kay. Now 76, Danny had just completed his 705th marathon. He was also sporting a new running shirt made especially for him, bearing the words 'Danny the Legend. 700+ marathons and counting.'

Rachel and I ran the whole of this year's marathon together and it was a thankfully uneventful race. Unlike the previous year, there were no flooded roads, no piggy backs, and no frantic searches for a suitable toilet stop for Rachel. We finished in 4h 11m, which was a new Cornish Marathon PB for both of us.

In addition to all the marathons we had completed together, Rachel also ran another two on her own, taking her total to 10 marathons in less than three years. I thought

43

it was about time she tried a new challenge.

'Do you want to run an ultramarathon with me?' I asked.

'An ultramarathon? Er... let me think... NO!'

'Why not?'

'I can't run an ultramarathon.'

'Of course you can.'

'No, I can't.'

'You said you couldn't do running. Then you said you couldn't do a 10k, a half-marathon, a marathon, triathlon, half-Ironman, 110-mile bike ride...'

'Yes, but that was different. An ultra is an ultra.'

'You'd love it. Let's do one together.'

'Nope. It's never gonna happen. '

I didn't take the hint and kept trying to persuade her by subtly dropping the idea into conversation. She stopped responding to my comments, which could have been her choosing to ignore me completely, but I took it as a sign that she was slowly warming to the idea.

My one and only ultramarathon had been the Endurancelife South Devon Coastal in 2016. My friend Mark and I battled 60mph winds, rain, hail and knee-deep mud, during the most ridiculous – but perversely enjoyable – event I have ever taken part in.

I happened to check the Endurancelife website a couple of weeks before this year's event in early February. The 10k, half-marathon and marathon distances had all sold-out weeks ago. But the ultra was listed as being 99% full. Surely that must be a sign? I booked the last two remaining places for Rachel and me before it was too late. Now all I needed was to find the right moment to break the news to her.

With so many other ultramarathons to choose from, it felt a bit unimaginative choosing the same event again. However, there were a lot of factors working in its favour. Firstly, Rachel knew I had completed it before, which hopefully meant she would feel it was achievable. At 35 (ish) miles, it is also a relatively short ultramarathon and therefore a gentle introduction into long distance trail running. But, with 6,500ft of climbing over mostly muddy and uneven terrain, it is far from easy. It is also not too far from where we live in Devon, making the route more familiar and the logistics of childcare far simpler.

When I told Rachel I had signed us both up, she just rolled her eyes and uttered a nonchalant 'ok', as though she had expected (or maybe even hoped) it was going to happen.

The event had a kit list of items we were required to carry with us for the duration of the race: mobile phone, money, foil blanket, head torch, hat, windproof jacket, first aid kit and enough food and water to fuel us for the day. Rachel made a trip to a local sports store and tried on a variety of running backpacks before settling on a fancy overpriced one that had been highly rated on some ultra-running forum. Having bought the bag, Rachel didn't try it on again until the morning of the race.

'It rubs a bit just under my arms,' she said.

'I thought you said it was really comfortable.'

'It was... in the shop. But I was wearing a thick coat at the time.'

Rachel's backpack contained a hydration bladder with a long tube to drink from while running. My hydration system consisted of two of our children's water bottles stuck into the side netting of my backpack. After filling her hydration bladder with two litres of water, Rachel then discovered that the seemingly spacious interior – which moments before she had been boasting about – was now predominantly filled with the full bladder of water. There was a tiny gap down the side in which she was able to squash her head torch, foil blanket and first aid kit, but she had no room for any of her food.

'Looks like you made a superb choice of bag,' I said, as I begrudgingly squashed her food into my bag.

We made our way to the race start and stood sheltering in the comparative warmth of the marquee. During Rachel's hourly checks of the weather forecast over the preceding 10 days, she had warned me of predicted torrential rain and high winds for the entire day. But then, on the morning of the race, the weather dramatically cleared. The wind dropped, and after a small bit of drizzle while we waited for the start, it stayed dry for the rest of the day. However, several weeks of heavy rain had already taken its toll on the ground, and the route was going to be extremely muddy and waterlogged.

A group of roughly 100 of us taking part in the ultramarathon assembled in a neighbouring tent for our race briefing. There were a few water stations and checkpoints interspersed along the route, but navigation of the course required us to follow signs rather than marshals. As there was also a marathon, half marathon and 10k event taking place, the routes and signs varied depending on which distance we were running.

'This is a sign that you will feel very happy to see,' said the organiser, holding up a sign saying ONE MILE TO GO.

There was an enthusiastic cheer from all those assembled.

'Unfortunately, for you ultrarunners, you will pass this sign TWICE.'

There was a collective laugh and groan from the crowd.

Rachel was surprisingly relaxed for someone about to begin her first ultramarathon. Looking around at the others, everyone else seemed equally calm. The start line of a road marathon tends to exhibit signs of nervousness in every direction. *Did I do enough training? Have I got enough gels? Do I start my watch when the gun goes off or when I cross the start line? Am I aiming for 9-minute miles or 12-minute miles?*

None of these are a concern at the start of an ultramarathon. *Did I do enough training?* We knew we hadn't done enough training. How do you train for a 35-mile run through mud? *Have I got enough gels?* I didn't have any gels; I just had a shitload of sandwiches and several bags of crisps. I had enough food to last for several days. *Do I start my watch when the gun goes off or when I cross the start line?* Who cares? We're going to be running for many hours and will not be concerned about precious seconds. Also, I didn't think my watch battery would last the distance, so started the Strava app on my phone before the race and buried it deep in my backpack and forgot about it. *Am I aiming for 9-minute miles or 12-minute miles?* We wouldn't be paying any attention to our speed. We were just aiming to see how far we could go and finishing the course would be a bonus. However long it took.

The starting horn sounded, and we headed diagonally up across the first field with the sea down below us to our left. After about 50 metres, those in front of us slowed to a walk, so I did too. Rachel turned to look at me to check whether this was allowed.

'You'd better get used to walking,' I said.

Runners slipped and slid down the next few hills, with those carrying walking poles using them like skiers to slalom their way down the slopes.

The first four miles passed without incident and Rachel appeared to be enjoying the occasion. But her mood soon deteriorated. The terrain along the coast path is either muddy or rocky, and it was frustrating for Rachel, who was used to running at a fairly decent pace on paved roads. She had not done a long trail run since the Salcombe Marathon nearly two years previously. The long uphill slogs and the treacherous descents took away everything Rachel enjoyed about running and added a sense of fear and apprehension in its place.

After eight miles, I could tell the rage had well and truly descended on Rachel. She became extremely quiet and resorted to monosyllabic answers to my questions and the occasional grunt. There were glimpses of this during both the Salcombe Marathon and the Barcelona Marathon, but on each of those occasions it was towards the end of the race. But now, we were not even a quarter of the way through, and I was daunted by the prospect of how Rachel was going to cope when we still had the distance of a full marathon to go.

I sensed anger and resentment in Rachel's manner, too. She had obviously agreed to take part in the ultra, but it was not without a fair amount of coaxing from me, and now I was being made to pay the price. Nothing I could say to Rachel seemed to help at all, and she talked about pulling out of the event.

'It's just not going to be possible for me to complete it,' she said.

'You will! We will!'

'HOW CAN YOU SAY THAT?' she shouted. 'We are not even a quarter of the way through, and we've been running for nearly two hours and it's horrible. I hate it. I shouldn't have agreed to do it.'

She didn't even respond to my subsequent words of encouragement. She slipped quickly into a deep decline. Metaphorically, of course. Things didn't end THAT badly.

The lead runners of the marathon distance, who had started their race 30 minutes after us, began skipping nimbly by, making running on such treacherous terrain appear effortless. Rachel's 'Good for Age' tag felt a very long time ago and she couldn't accept the fact that trail running was so different to road running.

To make matters worse, her stupid hydration backpack didn't even work properly. No amount of sucking on the valve at the end of the hose could produce anything more than the occasional drip of water. She was carrying two litres of water that she couldn't even drink. The only solution was to pull off the valve completely each time she wanted a drink and shove the tube in her mouth before the contents of the bladder spurted everywhere. This amused me greatly but made Rachel apoplectic.

I began to accept the fact that the race would probably end in a DNF for both of us. I was finding it extremely tough too and feeling pretty rubbish. And, although I knew I could probably struggle on and complete the distance, I didn't have the desire and couldn't really see the point. I had entered this race for Rachel and me to complete together. Having finished it before, I had nothing to prove to myself, and if Rachel decided to pull out, then I would

Did Not Start

happily do the same. I'm ashamed to say I even got a little excited about the prospect. It didn't take me long to warm to the idea of quitting, and I began to fantasise about what a relief I would feel to consciously take the decision to just give up and stop running. The thought was liberating and for the next few miles I secretly hoped that Rachel would get to the next checkpoint and decide to call it a day. Physically, she was more than capable of completing the race, but there was no chance she could survive the remaining miles with her current mindset. With my positivity drastically waning, too, there was little I could do to lift her spirits either.

We reached the checkpoint at Mill Bay at the end of the Kingsbridge Estuary, with beautiful views of the town of Salcombe across the water. This would be where our race ended. We would wait here for someone to give us a lift back to the start.

Two innocuous words from a race marshal changed all that.

'Nice t-shirt,' he said as we approached the checkpoint.

I looked down at the orange t-shirt I was wearing. It was the souvenir t-shirt from this same event two years previously. It was emblazoned with three words written big and bold.

NEVER GIVE UP.

My heart sank. I was already thinking about heading home and gaining a few bonus hours to relax later that day.

But how could I possibly throw in the towel while wearing a t-shirt with the words *NEVER GIVE UP*? Why did I decide to wear that stupid fucking t-shirt?

'Thanks,' I replied. 'I got it at a horrendous run I did a couple of years ago. And now I'm back for more!'

'That's the spirit,' he said.

I looked at Rachel. She was tucking into a handful of Jaffa Cakes and looking happier than I'd seen her in a while. As had been the case in the Dartmoor Classic, maybe she was just hungry?

'Are we going to continue?' I asked tentatively.

She shrugged her shoulders. 'We might as well, I guess.'

'Ok,' I smiled.

The suffering experienced during a physical challenge, such as a long run, swim or bike ride, is obviously very different to actual suffering experienced in life, whether it be through illness, trauma or grief. No matter how hard or painful a race feels, there is always the underlying knowledge that you signed yourself up for it. We only ever have ourselves to blame (or often, in Rachel's case, me). I am usually able to remind myself of this fact whenever I'm struggling, and it does tend to improve my mindset. In extreme circumstances, however, the awareness that the misery is self-imposed can result in a sort of existential crisis where you severely question how you could have ever possibly considered that signing up to something like this was a good idea. The benefit – or perhaps drawback,

Did Not Start

depending on your outlook – of these moments of introspection, is that they are usually very short-lived. Soon after crossing that finish line, you realise that signing up was the best idea you've ever had, and you are already looking out for the next challenge.

It was going to be a big ask for Rachel's mindset to stay positive for the remainder of the race, but it was definitely turning in the right direction.

As we trudged up the bridleway away from Mill Bay, the ground became even more muddy as we moved away from the sandiness of the coast path. We were running along the side of a field on a flat but particularly muddy section when I heard a shout and a squeal from behind me and turned to see Rachel sitting on the ground in the mud.

'Shit, are you ok?' I asked.

'Yes, I think so,' she said, and then let out a loud chuckle. 'I was just running along and then suddenly my foot slipped and here I am.'

I reached out my hand and helped her to her feet.

'Are you sure you're ok?'

'I'm fine. Is my backpack ok?'

'Your backpack? What do you mean?'

'Does it have any mud on it?'

'Er... why does it matter?'

'Because I want to take it back to the shop. It's a load of crap.'

'Your backpack is spotless,' I said.

'Good.'

Rachel's mood was buoyed considerably by her fall. She was back to her chatty, smiley and positive self and enjoying her running once again. The fall had highlighted the ridiculousness of the situation to her and reminded her that it was self-inflicted misery, and she shouldn't take it so seriously. From that moment onward, there was never any doubt that we would eventually reach the finish line.

For the previous few months, I had been thinking about trying to wean myself off energy gels. The boost in energy I had been feeling from them always seemed short-lived, and about twenty minutes after consuming a gel, my legs would feel devoid of energy once again. And the only way to overcome this was to take another gel. I interpreted this as my body's reaction to the overload of sugar and the subsequent crash that followed this spike in energy. It's probably more likely that I was lacking in fitness, but it was always preferable for me to blame the energy gels than to admit my own failings. But today marked the start of a no-gel experiment. Rather than gradually weaning myself off them, I was going cold turkey. It is an experiment I have continued up to the time of writing.

My cheese sandwiches had proved to be a real winner. I had cut them neatly into quarters and Rachel and I were eating one every four or five miles. My first packet of crisps, which I ate after about 12 miles, was possibly the greatest bag of crisps of my life. The humble salt and vinegar Hula Hoop had never tasted so good. I still didn't know if I could replicate this nutrition strategy in a road marathon, but I would try to find a way.

As we were running along an especially boggy and waterlogged stretch of bridleway near East Prawle, I heard another scream from Rachel behind me. I turned, expecting to see her lying on the floor again, but instead she was crouched next to a large muddy puddle in a tractor rut.

'What are you doing?' I asked.

'I was trying to have a drink and I dropped the valve for my hydration pack into there.'

'In that deep puddle? Are you serious?'

'Er... yes.'

'Of all the places you could have dropped it.'

'To be fair, most of the ground has looked like this.'

'That's true.'

Rachel had already dipped her hand into the puddle, forgetting to remove her glove, and failing to find the valve. She was using her other hand to squeeze the end of the water tube to stop it emptying the contents everywhere. I didn't have any gloves to get wet, so plunged both my hands into the icy water and began to rummage around in the mud at the bottom.

Several runners stepped around us but didn't seem in the least bit curious by the sight of us squatting next to a puddle, me with my arms submerged to the elbow in the brown water.

'Am I going to have to run the rest of the race holding this tube?' said Rachel.

'Got it!' I said after about 30 seconds, removing the mud-soaked valve from the puddle.

'Thank you! It's a good job it doesn't work. I'm not sure I would want to suck water through that.'

By this point, we had been joined by runners from the half marathon and the 10k, as our route merged with theirs. They had started a couple of hours after us and it made a pleasant change to be surrounded by other people for a while. Just as we were relishing the company of others, they all turned off at the ONE MILE TO GO sign and it went eerily quiet once again. It would be a very long time before we saw that sign again.

We had completed 18 miles, so were a little over halfway, and were both in good spirits and enjoying the experience. We ran through the village of Beeson and reached a road junction where a lady in a car pulled up with her window wound down. She was wearing a high-viz jacket, so we assumed she was a race official.

'Would you like a lift?' she asked.

'Err... no thanks,' I said.

'Ok,' she said. 'Nearly there.'

There was something in her manner that suggested she was a little confused about what we were doing and why we were out running where we were. She also seemed very surprised that we didn't want a lift. *Why would we want a lift?*

Did Not Start

Looking back, we should have realised that something was amiss.

It had been about 15 minutes since we had seen any other runners, but as we were towards the back of the race, this was to be expected. But we had seen no route markers either, and they had been very regular up until this point. The road then descended steeply into the village of Beesands, which I had not remembered doing during my previous race.

'Are you sure this is correct?' said Rachel.

'It must be,' I said, with no confidence. 'I don't see how we can have gone wrong. There will probably be a footpath off to the left any minute.'

As we rounded a bend at the bottom of the hill, we saw a marshal standing by a gatepost.

'Phew,' I said. 'Looks like we went the right way after all.'

'But isn't that the race finish?' said Rachel.

'Err... yeah. It looks like it.'

The marshal looked surprised to see us running towards him.

'Are we going the right way?' I asked.

'Sort of,' he said. 'You've just somehow come into the finish field from a different side, but you can come through this gate and the finish line is just over there.'

'But we are doing the Ultra. We've only done about 19 miles.'

'Oh,' he said, taking a big gulp. 'In that case, no, you are not going the right way. I think you must have missed a turn.'

Rachel and I looked at each other and then back up the long hill we had just run down unnecessarily. Our hearts sank. At that very moment, another marshal in a car pulled up alongside us.

'Everything alright?' he asked.

'These two are doing the ultra and must have missed a turning somewhere.'

'How far have you run?'

'About 19 miles, I think.'

'I know exactly where you went wrong. Hop in, I'll drop you off back at the turning.'

'Really? Are you sure? We are very muddy?'

'It's no trouble at all. Climb in.'

'Thank you so much,' we both said.

Sitting in that car for the five-minute ride back up the hill was a magical and very surreal experience.

'Do many runners make this mistake?' I asked.

'Er... no. You two are the only two I know of. And I've been marshalling this race every year since it started.'

'Oh.'

'Not to worry. I suppose it can be a bit tricky.'

'George did this same race a couple of years ago,' said Rachel from the back seat.

'Thanks for that, Rachel. You didn't spot the sign either!'

'Now, now, it's nobody's fault,' said the marshal.

Did Not Start

He pulled up at the junction where we went wrong and subtly pointed out the big yellow arrow we had somehow missed. We thanked him profusely, climbed out of the car, and jogged down the correct track, after a detour of an extra mile plus a five-minute car journey. For the next half an hour, we gradually overtook a handful of marathon route walkers who we had already passed before our slight deviation. They all did confused double-takes at us.

'Got a bit lost,' is all we said.

We both had a new lease of life. After the initial frustration of taking a wrong turn and embarrassingly having to get a lift, we were both then thoroughly amused by our own stupidity.

We reached the village of Stokenham and climbed up the steep lane and down the other side to Deer Bridge at the end of Slapton Ley Nature Reserve. This section is always muddy, and I had been running here with Rachel a few weeks previously when she had taken a nasty fall. When faced with a decision of treading on some exposed tree roots or deep mud, she had chosen the tree roots and slipped and landed hard on her hip. She could not run for a couple of weeks afterwards and, with memories of that injury still fresh in her mind, the choice between the deep mud and the exposed slippery tree roots presented itself to her once again. Rachel didn't even hesitate this time and plunged her feet straight into the mud.

When we eventually reached the village of Beesands

again (this time correctly), this marked the end of the run for those running the 28-mile 'marathon' distance. There was never any doubt that we would begin our final 7-mile loop to complete the ultra.

We plodded onward and upward and eventually reached the car park above Start Point lighthouse. On the previous occasion I had run the ultra, the wind and then hail had almost knocked us over and the race had been diverted inland for safety reasons.

Conditions were now perfect. As we followed the lane down to the lighthouse, the wind had dropped completely, the cloud had cleared, and with only a little over an hour until sunset, everything was cast in the golden hour's wondrous glow. For the final seven miles, we didn't see another runner. If the weather had been bad, or if either of us had been running alone, it might have felt a little lonely or eerie. But having been within sight or sound of many other runners all day – except for when we got lost – it was strangely magical.

As we ran down the last field towards the finish line, the organisers were already in the process of packing away the race HQ. We crossed what was left of the line in a time of 8h 28m.

James, the race director, stopped what he was doing and came and shook our hands and congratulated us both. We thanked him for putting on such a fabulous event and asked him to pass on our thanks to the marshal who gave us a lift.

Did Not Start

'Ah, so you were the two who got a bit lost? I heard about that on the radio.'

'YOU HEARD IT ON THE RADIO?' said Rachel, a little shocked.

'No! Just the race radios, I mean. These walkie talkies that the staff use to communicate during the race.'

'Oh, thank god for that! I thought you meant the radio radio. That would have been even more embarrassing.'

There was one other finisher after us, which surprised us as we had assumed we were last. Not that we would have had any problem at all with finishing last. In fact, there is something very admirable about coming last. Being on your feet for longer than everyone else, not having the company of other runners, and coping with the perceived feeling that you are holding everyone up. 86 runners started the ultra and 26 of them pulled out at different stages before the finish, so we both felt very proud of our accomplishment.

'You're an ultrarunner,' I said to Rachel as we tottered back to the car.

'That sounds very weird. Say it again.'

'You are an ultrarunner!'

'It sounds even better the second time. I can't quite believe it. Thanks for running with me and convincing me to give it a go. Even if you did take a wrong turn and make us run further than we needed to.'

'You took the wrong turn too.'

'Fair enough. I'm glad it wasn't mentioned on the radio. That would have been weird. And don't write about it in one of your books, ok?'

FIVE

During the 11 years we lived in Northampton, we all became very close to our elderly neighbour Doug. For 18 months after moving to Devon, while still working as a photographer, I drove back to Northampton a couple of times a month to fulfil all my remaining wedding bookings. Each time I was back in the county, I would call in to see Doug, his wife Christine, and our old cat Father Dougal whom we left with Doug and Christine when we moved to Devon.

After photographing my final wedding at the end of 2014, visits became a lot more infrequent, and we only tended to be back in Northampton once or twice a year at most. But we kept in contact with Doug regularly on the phone, filling him in on what we had all been up to, and discussing the latest results of Northampton Town Football Club.

During one phone call, Doug casually dropped into conversation that he was going into hospital later that week for a little procedure. When I pried further, he disclosed that he had recently been diagnosed with pancreatic cancer.

He said he hadn't wanted to burden us with it which was why he had not told us before. Doug was in his mid-seventies, but doctors were optimistic with his prognosis as he had been diagnosed fairly early and was therefore eligible for surgery.

A few days later, I made a surprise visit to Northampton to see Doug in hospital after his surgery. When I found him in his ward he was laughing and joking with one of the nursing staff and the man in the next bed.

'Oh my word! Look who it is!' he said when he saw me enter the ward.

'Hey Doug. Look at you! You're looking great.'

'I feel incredible! It's so lovely to see you, kiddo. You didn't come all this way from Devon just to see me, did you?'

'As if I would come all this way for you, Doug,' I smiled. 'I just happened to be passing.'

'Ha, well it's really great to see you, kiddo.'

Doug had been on the ward less than 24 hours and already knew the names of the other five patients and all of the different members of staff. The operation had been a success and Doug would soon begin an intensive period of chemotherapy and the doctors were hopeful for his outlook.

We sat and chatted for about an hour and Doug filled me in on the life stories of the other patients and I told him all about our recent ultramarathon. When visiting time came to an end, I said goodbye to Doug and went to meet

Did Not Start

up with some friends for a curry and a few beers. I stayed the night with my friend Damo (who claims his grandma invented Banoffee Pie), and then drove back down to Devon the following morning.

There was a shout from outside our house later that day and Rachel opened the door to find a delivery driver holding our cat Moomin. The woman was in tears and explained that as she was heading back out onto the road after delivering a parcel to us, she had seen Moomin get hit by a van and then stagger through a gateway into a field. The other vehicle hadn't stopped, so the delivery driver went and located Moomin hiding behind the wall. Knowing she was ours after seeing her on delivery rounds, she brought her straight to us.

Moomin was alive but in a very bad way. There was a lot of blood on her face. A large section of skin and fur was hanging off and her jaw was certainly not as it should be. She tried to escape the delivery driver's arms, so she placed her down on the kitchen floor and Moomin staggered and hid behind the fridge, unable to put any weight on her front right leg and bumping into things clumsily along the way.

I grabbed our cat carrier from the shed, retrieved Moomin from behind the fridge, thanked the delivery driver for bringing her to us, and left her and Rachel consoling each other as I drove quickly to our local vet.

The vet took Moomin from me immediately and told

me they would do what they could and would be in touch. An hour later we had to pick the kids up from school and let them know what had happened and that there was a strong chance Moomin might not make it. They were all distraught and we waited by the phone that evening for an update. At about 6pm, the vet phoned to say Moomin had undergone emergency surgery to wire her jaw back together, and they had stitched the skin on her chin as best as possible. They would keep her in overnight, but all being well, we could collect her the following morning.

The kids went to school the next day, excited about the prospect of seeing Moomin later. She didn't look like the same cat when I went to collect her that morning. It wasn't just the obvious physical damage that the accident had caused; a piece of prominent wire wrapped around her lower jaw, and the skin around her chin all clotted and raw. Her whole persona seemed to have changed. Her head and shoulders drooped, the spark from her eyes was gone and her brow was furrowed. Basically, she looked mightily pissed off. Which was understandable considering the circumstances. The vet was very pleased with how the operation had gone but was a little concerned that she still wasn't weight bearing on one of her front legs. They had x-rayed and examined her and found no sign of any damage to the leg but told us to keep an eye on it as there was a possibility it was a neurological issue.

We were told to feed her very soft food for a few days to give her jaw the best chance of healing, so when we got

Did Not Start

home Rachel offered her some soft scrambled eggs and tuna fish. Both of which Moomin refused and then hobbled off to hide behind the fridge.

The children were delighted to see Moomin, despite the fact she didn't seem the same cat as before, and we tried to reassure them it would take a while for her to fully recover.

Over the following days, things didn't look good. Moomin was still not using her front right leg correctly, with it folding over at the joint as she walked. She was also refusing to eat all of the soft foods we offered her. We took her back to the vets and there was a suggestion that if she didn't start using her leg soon, they may need to amputate. And if she was unable to eat then she may have to spend the rest of her life being fed by syringe. We were prepared to do all that was necessary, but we did start to wonder what sort of quality-of-life Moomin would lead and whether perhaps it hadn't been so lucky that she had escaped death after all.

She had lost a lot of weight and was looking more and more feeble. We had to break the news to the children that Moomin was far from being out of the woods yet. She had shown a vague interest in all the foods we had offered her but seemed to be struggling to co-ordinate the softer textures of food and her new facial arrangement.

'Can I try giving her some of her normal cat biscuits?' I said to Rachel.

'I don't think that's a good idea. The vet said soft food. She's just had her jaw wired.'

'I know, but soft food isn't working. She's not eating anything. We haven't got much to lose.'

'I suppose it's worth a try.'

I put down a small bowl of biscuits in front of Moomin and she began tucking in veraciously. It was pretty stressful to watch as she seemed completely unfazed by the fact her jaw was wired together. She couldn't get enough of the biscuits and after a few minutes the bowl was empty. Maybe she found the size and shape easier to get into her mouth, or maybe it was the familiarity of her favourite food, but within a couple of days she had put on a bit of weight and gradually over the next week began using her right leg correctly. By the time the vet removed the wire from her jaw, she had made a complete recovery.

Moomin's recuperation coincided with a period of extreme weather in the UK, which made her less inclined to head off on her usual adventures. Despite regular winter storms since moving to Devon five years previously, we had not seen so much as a single snowflake settle on the ground. While other parts of the UK seemed to get some snow most years, the South West – because of its slightly warmer climate – remained largely untouched.

We enjoyed some brilliant snow days with Layla, Leo and Kitty in Northampton when they were much younger, but every winter since had ended in disappointment. 2018 looked like it was heading that same way too. February was all but over; the daffodils had bloomed early and spring seemed to have well and truly sprung.

And then The Beast from the East hit Great Britain. Anticyclone Hartmu – to give it its official (boring) name – brought widespread heavy snowfall across many parts of Europe. On this occasion, the South West was hit worst (or best, depending on your outlook) by the snowstorm. Schools were closed for several days; supermarket shelves were bare and many of our local roads were impassable. And we loved every second of it. We made the most of the steep Devon hills with sledges and body boards, and there was a sense of childlike enthusiasm in everyone we met, particularly among proper Devon locals (of which I will never be one), many of whom had never experienced proper snow. Our landlords had lived on the farm where we live for over 70 years and never seen snow like it.

Some of Layla's friends turned up unexpectedly at our house on one morning with their parents to go sledging on nearby hills. After a fun few hours, we made hot chocolates for the children back at our house and then decided to crack open a magnum of red wine (for the parents, not Layla's friends) that we had been saving for a special occasion. It was 1pm on a school day and we had been sledging all morning. It was definitely a special occasion.

My weekly Dad's football on the Sunday morning went ahead as normal. A fresh dump of snow arrived, and with the roads not suitable for driving or cycling, I walked the three miles to the all-weather pitch, excited about the novelty of playing football in the snow, and to test whether it really was all-weather. I expected there to be a small handful of players there from our usual gathering of about 15, but when I arrived, I discovered 22 grown men had made the trip – our biggest ever turnout – all excited about the prospect of playing football in the snow. It turned out the pitch was almost unplayable, but it was brilliant fun anyway.

The high banked Devon lanes meant there were some stretches of road where the north-facing side didn't get any winter sun and the snow lingered for several weeks. Just as it had almost all melted, the Beast from the East made a return in mid-March, and we got to experience it all for a second time.

Did Not Start

SIX

With travel across the country heavily disrupted because of the Beast from the East, Rachel and I were grateful that things were back to normal by April.

Our two previous European marathons – Rome and Barcelona – had been whistle-stop two-night trips. This year, Rachel and I were running the Paris Marathon. And this time we had the luxury of an extra night. We left Devon late Friday morning, caught a train to London Paddington, a connection to St Pancras, and were in Paris by early evening without leaving the ground.

Our quaint little boutique hotel was bordered on either side by sex shops selling dildos in the shape of the Eiffel Tower. We wandered along Boulevard de Clichy until we reached the unmistakable red windmill of the Moulin Rouge; its spectacular sails glowing bright against the night sky. As we stood and gaped open-mouthed from the other side of the road, a waiter offered us an outside table at his restaurant. I was instinctively about to thank him and move on, when I realised I was extremely hungry, and eating in the shadow of the Moulin Rouge didn't seem like such a bad idea at all.

I looked at Rachel. She nodded.

'Oui, merci monsieur,' I said.

We were sitting at a busy intersection opposite one of the most popular sights in Paris. Our expectations for the meal were set pretty low, as this was tourist central. We ordered a burger and a baked camembert salad to share. Both were incredible. Unlike our previous marathons in Edinburgh, Rome and Barcelona, we had arrived in Paris two nights before the marathon rather than one, so could eat and drink on our first night without the added pressure of the following day's marathon hanging over us.

It was a fascinating place to sit and people-watch. There were many Parisians walking home at the end of their working week; groups of locals out for an early evening walk; tourists from all over the world, and many who were clearly visiting Paris for the marathon, choosing to broadcast to everyone how awesome they were by parading around the city at night in their shorts and compression socks.

My only previous memory of Paris was a traumatic experience as a child getting lost in a hotel during a family holiday. Rachel's only other visit had been part of a stay with her evil French pen pal, so we both had various negative associations with the city, which we were keen to shake off.

After a long leisurely hotel breakfast the following

Did Not Start

morning, we set off from our hotel and weaved our way through the quiet Saturday morning back streets until we popped out at the Louvre.

'Shall we go in?' I asked Rachel.

'I suppose we should. We are not likely to be back in Paris anytime soon. Do you want to?'

'Yeah, I guess we should.'

We walked around the famous glass pyramid featured as the backdrop in blockbuster films such as *The Da Vinci Code* and *The Bourne Identity*, and then came across an unmoving queue that snaked endlessly.

'I'm really not that bothered about going in. Are you? It's such a nice day,' I said.

'Me neither. Which famous paintings are in the Louvre anyway?'

'The Mona Lisa. Only the most famous painting in the world.'

'Oh. Maybe we should queue then.'

I pulled out my phone, adamant that I wasn't going to spend my day in Paris standing in line to see a painting. I googled Mona Lisa, and thousands of images of the famous painting appeared – as you would expect they would. You know how Google works.

'There you go,' I said, showing the phone to Rachel. 'Now we can say we've been to the Louvre and seen the Mona Lisa.'

'Amazing. And we didn't even have to queue.'

We spent the morning lazily following the banks of the Seine, stopping for coffee and then minutes afterwards beginning a desperate search for a toilet after over-enthusiastically hydrating in preparation for tomorrow's marathon.

Rachel's good friend Emma had visited Paris recently and lent us her guidebook with a list of her recommendations. Top of the handwritten list, and written in bold, capital letters, underlined, with plenty of exclamation marks were three words: *LE MARAIS – FALAFEL!!!!!!!*

Once a popular neighbourhood for French nobility and aristocrats, Le Marais fell out of favour and into disrepair after the French Revolution. It wasn't until the late 1970s and early 1980s that Le Marais began its own revolution. Brought about largely because of the area's popularity within the LGBT community, Le Marais is now a bustling collection of trendy bars, restaurants, galleries, bakeries and boutique shops.

But it wasn't just Le Marais that Emma wanted us to visit. The highlight of Emma's visit to Le Marais – and seemingly her entire trip to Paris – was, by the sounds of things, a falafel.

'A falafel? In Paris?' I questioned when Rachel read Emma's note.

'Yes! Why is that weird?'

'Isn't falafel middle-eastern? It's not really a food you

tend to associate with France.'

'Well, Emma seems to think it is worth it.'

'Emma is vegan, isn't she?'

'No, she eats chicken sometimes.'

'Oh yeah, she's a chicken-eating vegan.'

'No, she's not. But anyway, what's that got to do with it?'

'The French are famous for their food – steaks, cheese, frogs' legs, snails.'

'So you're saying that the falafel aren't any good and Emma is lying?'

'No, of course I'm not saying she's lying! I'm saying that the falafel in Paris might be amazing... if you are a vegan. Or even a chicken-eating vegan.'

'Well, what do you want to eat for lunch then? Frogs' legs? Snails?'

'Well, no, I really fancy a falafel actually, now you mention it.'

La Rue de Rosiers in Le Marais was busy with tourists and Parisians roaming the streets, and most of them seemed to be eating falafel. Those who weren't eating falafel were queueing for falafel. Every other shop was a falafel shop. They have completely taken over this part of the city. And I don't think it was just the vegans.

We picked a restaurant that looked popular because it had a fair queue of people at the takeaway window. A queue outside a restaurant proves that either the food is extremely popular, or the service is exceptionally slow. I realise I have double standards: I won't queue to see the world's most famous painting, but I'll happily stand in line for some deep-fried chickpeas.

'You're brave having falafel the day before a marathon,' I said.

'Well, Emma said we should have one. Can you ask for mine not to be too spicy?'

'And how am I supposed to do that? You've heard how bad my French is.'

'I don't know. Maybe point at the picture of the chili pepper and shake your head?'

'Thanks. Now you're getting me to be a mime artist.'

The falafel were delicious. Not in the least bit French, but delicious, nonetheless. I would definitely include it on my own list of things to do in Paris.

After leaving Le Marais, we crossed the river, walked past Notre Dame, and through the beautifully landscaped park of Le Jardin du Luxembourg. Frustratingly, people are prohibited from sitting on most of the lawns in these gardens, but chairs are lined up in rows around the park so visitors can sit and admire the grass instead. Rachel and I had another coffee and watched people sailing toy boats in the lake in front of the palace. We felt like we should at least visit one art gallery while in Paris, so left the park and eventually reached the Museum de Orsay just in time for last admission.

'I think I've done some serious damage to my legs,' said Rachel.

Did Not Start

'What's wrong?'

'I don't know. I've got shooting pains on the front of my right leg. I think I've got shin splints from walking too far.'

I glanced at my GPS watch. We had walked almost 13 miles around Paris, which was, in hindsight, a bit of a stupid thing to do the day before a marathon, and perhaps not advisable. But travelling to Paris and spending our only full free day resting when there were so many sights to see seemed like a waste.

'I'm sure you'll be ok. We can just walk slowly around the gallery and then get the metro or a taxi back to the hotel.'

'I think it's too late. The damage is already done.'

'You'll be fine. You often have a mystery injury the day before a marathon.'

'A MYSTERY INJURY? What are you talking about? Are you saying I'm being a hypochondriac?'

'What? No! Of course not. Sorry, I just meant that I think you'll be ok tomorrow.'

'Well, I don't think we should go around the art gallery. I can hardly even walk. Sorry.'

'That's ok. I wasn't that bothered, anyway. We can just look at the Monets and Van Goghs on our phones from outside. It's free.'

We sat on the steps outside the Museum de Orsay in the sunshine, listening to an elderly violinist busker, secretly relieved that we had dodged another art gallery.

Rachel continued to massage her lower leg with concern so we caught the Metro back to our hotel in the hope she would recover before the marathon.

Later that evening, we went to a nearby Italian restaurant for dinner (when in Paris...) to do some pre-marathon carb-loading. Rachel had come a long way since her days of being a notoriously fussy eater before running events. The night before her first marathon in Edinburgh a few years previously, I had bought a packet of instant rice – naively thinking food could not get any simpler – and she had rejected it because it contained coriander. Despite being a herb, coriander was vetoed by Rachel as it has an association with spicy dishes. But she had become a bit more relaxed since then, having ham, egg and chips the night before the Barnstaple Marathon and then pinchos and beer in Barcelona. Ever since, however, she had regretted the pinchos and decided they were part of the reason for what she considered a sub-par performance in the marathon. In Paris, she decided to play it safe again.

I ordered a big plate of lasagne, fries and salad, and Rachel opted for spaghetti with tomato sauce (a step up from plain pasta at least). It arrived garnished with basil.

'Look, it's got basil on it!' I said with mock shock.

'Stop being a dick, George.'

'But basil is a herb. You're not going to eat that, are you?'

'Of course I'm going to eat it. I'm not as bad as I used

to be. I ate falafel for lunch, didn't I?'

'Some of it, yes. Although you made me eat the cucumber and the cabbage because you were worried what they might do to you.'

We ate a substantial hotel breakfast on the morning of the marathon, before a two-mile walk to the start of the race. Rachel's leg felt fine and her severe case of maranoia had been miraculously cured once again.

It was a bright, spring morning and the forecast looked good. When we arrived at the start, there seemed to be a distinct lack of portable toilets, so we slipped into a nearby McDonald's and joined a queue of runners who were doing the same.

When we reached the front of the queue, a security guard asked for our token.

'Token?' I said.

'Oui.'

He then explained that tokens were given to people who had bought a McDonald's breakfast. By this point I was absolutely bursting for a McWee so pleaded with the security guard in my awful French and did the international mime to show I was about to wet myself (jumping up and down with my hands on my crotch), and he eventually let us both in. I have eaten enough McDonald's in my life to be worthy of a VIP toilet pass, so I didn't feel guilty.

With 50,000 runners taking on the 26.2 miles, the Paris

Marathon is one of the biggest in the world. As we stood in our starting pen, I looked at the thousands of runners stretched ahead of us down the Champs-Élysées, and behind us all the way back towards the Arc de Triomphe standing boldly behind us, and I felt honoured to be part of such a tremendous spectacle.

There is no vetting process for running events. You don't have to prove you are any good at running, or even that you can run. The more popular marathons use a ballot system when the number of entries outnumbers the places, but it is a completely open and inclusive entry process.

Running events are unique in this respect, and I can't think of any other sport where absolute amateurs compete alongside the very best in the world. At most of the big city marathons, elite runners such as Eliud Kipchoge will run the same route, pass the same drink stations, step in the same puddles as 74-year-old Brenda from Woking who is taking part in her first ever marathon. And Steve, the army-veteran wheelchair user, will follow the identical route of the women's world record holder Mary Kittany. It would be a bit like turning up at your local tennis courts for a game of doubles and being paired with Serena Williams; or arriving at your weekly five-aside football match and discovering you're playing against Cristiano Ronaldo.

Professional cyclists do take part in some of the bigger mass-participation sportives, but these are not considered high-profile events on the cycling calendar. The big city marathons – especially the six World Marathon Majors:

Did Not Start

London, New York, Boston, Chicago, Berlin and Tokyo – are right up there with the Olympics and World Championships on the athletics calendar.

This level playing field for athletes does throw up the occasional surprise. In 2017, 23-year-old Josh Griffiths turned up at the start line of the London Marathon, having never taken part in a race over the distance before. He was the first British male to cross the finish line, securing a place in the national team at the World Championships. In the 2018 Boston Marathon, unknown runner Sarah Sellers – a full-time nurse from Arizona – finished second in the women's race, walking away (or perhaps hobbling) with $75,000 in prize money.

The starting gun sounded, and we began our slow trudge towards the start line. With 50,000 runners all starting their race from the same place, the first few miles did feel quite congested. Rachel and I were in no hurry, though, and happy to soak up the atmosphere.

Paris is a very well-supported marathon, with an estimated 250,000 spectators along the route. We ran around the Place de la Concorde – Paris's biggest square and the site of many notable executions in France's history, including King Louis XVI and Marie Antoinette. As we skirted the edge of le Marais district, the crowds were cheering from the roadside and of course clutching their early morning falafel.

We continued along Rue de Rivoli and around the Place

de la Bastille – the location of the Bastille prison until it was stormed during the French Revolution in 1789. Southeast along wide Parisian boulevards we ran, before completing a large loop of Bois de Vincennes – the largest public park in Paris. This mid-section of the marathon made a nice peaceful contrast to the liveliness and hubbub of the busy city centre streets.

Although we had seen a vast amount of Paris on our extensive walking tour the day before, running a marathon is a really great way to see the main sights of a city, as well as many of the less-popular parts. And by less-popular, I of course mean crap. But it is by seeing all of these different aspects – the crap parts as well as the popular – that you build up a better rapport with a city. And during our brief stay, Rachel and I had both grown very fond of Paris. Particularly its falafel.

After completing our loop of the park, the route then headed back west, following the banks of the river Seine for about six miles with wonderful views of many of Paris's most iconic sights including Notre Dame and the Eiffel Tower. The sun was shining, but I had bought a new baseball cap with *PARIS* embroidered on the peak, with a picture of the Eiffel Tower – just like all Parisians wear, no doubt.

After about 19 miles, Rachel decided she needed the toilet. We passed a row of portable toilets at a drinks station, and I suggested she stop and use them.

'No, it's ok. I'll try and hold it.'

About a minute later, she decided she couldn't possibly hold it, so spent the next two miles scouting out any other possible places to go. We then passed another portable toilet on the other side of a barrier. In her desperation, Rachel straddled the fence and found the toilet locked, so disappeared into a nearby bush. At about the 22-mile point, she then started getting stomach cramps, so we ended up walking a good chunk of the final four miles.

'You shouldn't have eaten that basil,' I said.

'Stop being such a dick, George.'

Karma had its way shortly after. As we broke into a gentle run again, we reached a bit of a bottleneck as the road narrowed, and I tried to step up and over a curb to pass a runner who was walking. My tired legs had other ideas and my toe caught an uneven paving slab. I tumbled forwards, breaking my fall with my hands in the gravel.

'Ça va?' said the runner behind me as I jumped to my feet.

'Oui, ça va bien, merci.'

'Are you alright?' said Rachel.

'Yes, it was my own fault,' I said, wiping my bloody hands on my shorts.

With four miles to go, we had been comfortably on target for a sub-4-hour marathon. After her stomach issues, Rachel had encouraged me to go ahead. But I had been secretly relieved to walk, and, as I had demonstrated with my inability to control my legs properly, I was not in great shape either. Perhaps walking 13 miles the previous day had taken its toll on both of us. Or maybe there was basil in my lasagne.

The final few miles of the marathon route left the city streets and entered the extensive park of Bois de Boulogne. Like the Bois de Vincennes which we ran through on the eastern side of Paris, this park was also created by the first president (and final monarch) of France, Napoleon III in the 1850s and 1860s. He is said to have been inspired by his time living in London, and Paris has certainly benefited from these immense green spaces.

As we turned the last corner onto Avenue Foch (stop it!), the Arc de Triomphe came into view and we both gave little squeals of delight. It was a wonderful end to the marathon, and as we crossed the finish line, neither of us were in the least bit bothered we were 11 minutes over the four-hour mark. That was 11 minutes more sightseeing.

That evening, we walked our weary legs up the hill behind the Moulin Rouge into the Montmartre district, with the beautiful white domes of the Sacré-Cœur Basilica on its summit. Rachel cursed me the entire way up for stupidly insisting on having dinner at the highest point in Paris. But all was forgiven when we found an outside table at a restaurant bordering a beautiful town square. We squashed our chairs next to each other and ate delicious, overpriced steak frites and drank delicious, overpriced wine. It was the perfect spot to people watch and worth every euro, as families, couples, artists, tourists and locals all wandered the streets like extras in a film.

There were two men – both in their thirties – sat at the table next to us. They too sat on the same side of the table so that they could look out onto the square. They weren't eating, but during the time we were there, they went through three bottles of red wine together without uttering a single word to each other. They kept each other's glasses topped up and both looked utterly content with their situation. It looked like a damn good lads' night out, and there was something wonderfully Parisian about it.

We had only been in Paris for three nights, and despite not visiting a single museum or gallery, we had covered well over 40 miles of its streets on foot, so felt like we had made the most of our short visit. As we caught the Eurostar back to England the following day, all traumatic childhood memories of Paris had been replaced by much fonder ones.

SEVEN

A year earlier, Rachel had achieved a finishing time at the Exeter Marathon that was fast enough to allow her to qualify for the London Marathon via a Good for Age place. This meant she did not have to rely on the overly subscribed main ballot. It had been a personal challenge of Rachel's to try to achieve the badge of honour of being 'Good for Age'. There is not an actual badge, although I think Rachel would have liked one. She had not shown any real desire to run London, feeling it was a bit too big and commercial, but she also did not want to turn down the opportunity. The closer it got to marathon day, the more excited Rachel became. I had tried and failed again to get a place through the ballot.

Marathon weekend arrived and the five of us drove to London on the Saturday night to stay with my sister. Despite owning drawers full of different running kit, Rachel announced just before we left home that she had nothing suitable to wear for the race.

'What about your usual running vest?' I asked.

'No, it's too clingy and the forecast is very hot.'

Did Not Start

'What about that one?'

'No, I don't like the colour.'

'That one?'

'I don't like the feel.'

'What about the yellow one?'

'Too baggy.'

'The purple one?'

'Too purple.'

'That one?'

'Meh.'

So, I jokingly suggested she could borrow my running vest that I had worn only once during my Ironman run, before ceremoniously retiring it. She tried it on.

'This is perfect,' she said. 'It's just what I've been after. Do you mind if I borrow it?'

'Not at all. To be fair, it looks a lot better on you than it did on me.'

The following morning, Layla, Leo and Kitty got to spend some time with their cousins, before we drove Rachel as close as we could get her to the marathon start at Blackheath. With over 40,000 runners taking part, the London Marathon start is spread across three different sites, with all three eventually merging between miles two and three once the field has spread out a little.

After wishing Rachel luck, we drove and parked in Deptford and walked a short distance to join the marathon route. Deptford is not as scenic as neighbouring

Greenwich, where spectators have the Cutty Sark as a backdrop. Our backdrop was a cafe called Booze & Burrito. Unfortunately, it was closed, otherwise it might have been a nice place to take the kids for a family breakfast. But Deptford was nice and quiet, and there was plenty of space for us to get a good view of the runners when they passed.

'I don't feel very well,' said Layla.

'Maybe you're just hungry?' I said. 'We'll get some food in a bit.'

Layla didn't answer, which was unusual for her.

The main field of runners was not expected any time soon, but minutes after we took our positions by the roadside, the first of the wheelchair racers powered by at an astonishing speed. The blind runners followed soon after, attached to their guides. And then a few minutes later the elite men came into view. It was the first time I had witnessed elite runners in real life, and I was overwhelmed by their speed. I think I could possibly have kept up with them for about 50 metres before my lungs gave out. They were going to be sustaining this pace for 26.2 miles.

Mo Farah – competing in his first marathon since he retired from track running – was looking focused and determined as he passed. Despite a later mix-up at a drinks station when he had to run back to get a different bottle, he went on to finish third, setting a new British record in the process.

'Wasn't that incredible? Did you see the speed they were

Did Not Start

running at?' I said to Layla, Leo and Kitty.

'It wasn't that fast,' said Kitty. 'I could probably go as fast as they were.'

'Yeah, me too,' said Leo, and he and Kitty sprinted up the road.

'See!' said Kitty.

'Yeah, that was quite quick, but you both look exhausted, and you ran about 10 metres.'

'Whatever,' said Leo.

'Did you think they were fast, Layla?' I asked, concerned that she was still quiet.

'Not really,' she muttered.

'How are you feeling?'

'Awful.'

'We've got a little while before Mummy will come through here. Let's go and get something to eat.'

There was a convenience store close by (how convenient), so we called inside to buy some pastries and snacks.

'Dad, I really don't feel very well...' said Layla, before projectile vomiting in the middle of the aisle.

'Oh wow, you really aren't well. Poor old you.'

A kind member of staff came over. I apologised for the mess and offered to help clear it up, but she told me it was fine and to leave her to it. We quickly paid for our stuff and went back outside so that Layla could get some fresh air.

'How do you feel now?' I asked.

'A bit better, I think.'

'Sit down on the floor for a while and try to drink some of your water.'

A few minutes later, we heard some shouting behind us and turned to see a man running from the store clutching an armful of bottles of spirits. The alarm was sounding, and he was being chased by a security guard and the same member of staff who moments earlier had been cleaning up Layla's sick. The thief disappeared up a side alley and the security guard and the staff member decided not to give chase.

'That poor lady isn't having the best start to her day,' I said.

Some friends of ours from home soon joined us at the roadside. They had come all the way from Devon for the weekend to watch the marathon, and specifically Rachel.

'Sorry we are late. Have we missed anything?' said Cath.

'Not really,' I said. 'Just Mo Farah, blind runners, wheelchairs, Layla being sick in Tesco Express, and a shoplifting incident. And we've only been here 15 minutes.'

'Wow, busy morning so far. Has Rachel been past yet?'

'Not yet. I think she'll be through here any second.'

Just a couple of minutes later, Rachel came into view. She saw us at the roadside and began waving frantically.

'Go Rachel... Go Mummy... Well done... Keep going,' we all shouted, and she high-fived us as she passed.

'Was Rachel wearing your running vest?' asked Cath.

'Er, yes, apparently she doesn't own any suitable running tops.'

She raised her eyebrows in surprise.

'No, I don't understand either,' I said.

From Deptford, we walked to the Docklands Light Railway and took the train over to the glamorously named Mudchute on the even more glamorously named Isle of Dogs. In case you are wondering (I was), Mudchute got its name from being the dumping ground for all the silt and waste during the construction of the Millwall Docks in the 1860s. The origin of the Isle of Dogs is less clear. The name has been used since the early 1500s, and some say it was where former Kings or Queens of England kept their hunting dogs. However, there is little evidence to corroborate this.

Layla was feeling a little better, so we bought sandwiches and a massive tray of grapes and found a good vantage point of the marathon route from the top of some steps.

I have always loved watching the London Marathon on television, but this was my first time spectating in real life. I took part in the event in 2009 – my first ever marathon – and regret not making the most of the occasion. My focus was too heavily on my finishing time, and I neglected to fully appreciate the spectacle. I have entered (and been rejected by) the ballot every year since and will certainly make the most of it if I ever get a chance to run it again.

Despite finding little enjoyment from my first marathon, I was overwhelmed by the vast crowds. Almost every inch of the course is lined with spectators, all choosing to spend their day at the roadside, clapping and cheering at runners. The London Marathon bib number displays the runners' names, too, and the first time someone shouted, 'GO GEORGE' I looked around thinking, '*who? ME?*' It was an empowering feeling and certainly helped lift my spirits. By about the 24-mile point, however, when my legs had turned to mush, the novelty of people shouting my name had well and truly worn off. It became a struggle to force a smile at each shout of my name.

I was desperate for the race to be over, but I remember still feeling awestruck about the dedication of the spectators, and of how boring it must be to stand there for hours on end, cheering and clapping at random strangers. And they don't even get the benefit of the medal and goody bag at the end.

But spectating a big city marathon is far from boring. Standing at the roadside, waiting for Rachel to pass, was an amazing experience. I loved every minute and could happily have stood there for the duration. It is people watching on an extreme scale. It is impossible not to be caught up in the occasion; thousands of runners, of all ages, shapes and sizes; each with different stories to tell;

Did Not Start

different reasons and motivations that brought them to that start line. Some make it look effortless. Others make it clearly apparent that it is the hardest thing they have ever attempted. And it's not just tiring for the runners. Being a spectator at a big city marathon is utterly exhausting. Your eyes are constantly scanning the runners, trying to spot the person or persons you have come to support. You can't take your eyes off the course for a second in case you miss them. And when coupled with all the clapping and cheering, you feel you can partly empathise with the runners' fatigue.

We positioned ourselves somewhere between the 16 and 17-mile markers, and Rachel passed us looking like she was fully embracing the experience. It was the hottest London Marathon on record, and with the Paris Marathon only two weeks previously, Rachel was not trying for a PB and wanted to enjoy the occasion as much as possible. The grin across her face showed she was certainly doing just that. According to the online tracker, she was bang on four-hour pace. We stayed around for another hour, cheering on the other runners, and then headed back over the river to our car.

As we drove across London to meet Rachel, I noticed the occasional car driver flash their lights at me. I thought they were perhaps warning me of a police speed trap, but as I was driving at between 5 and 10mph, this seemed unlikely. I then assumed I was being paranoid, and it must be the sun glinting off their cars. Then, eight miles into our journey, a van pulled up alongside us at some traffic lights. The lady in the passenger seat signalled for me to wind down my window.

'You've got some grapes on your roof, mate,' she said.

I got out, and sure enough, our big cardboard tray of half-eaten grapes was sitting on the roof, wedged against the roof bars and had happily travelled eight miles across London with us after I had inadvertently left them there while loading the car.

'Oh god, Dad, you are SO embarrassing,' said Layla, who was clearly feeling back to normal.

EIGHT

It felt like my days of running road marathons with Rachel were numbered.

As well as her London Marathon, Rachel had now completed a handful of others without me. She had asked – half-heartedly – if I wanted to join her, but each time I had declined. It felt that, for now at least, she was on a different level to me and if we were to run together, then I would only hold her back. But at least we had Paris. We'll always have Paris.

After a couple of years struggling with sciatica and doing very little about it, I finally booked a session with a physiotherapist to see if he could do anything to help. After talking me through a series of exercises and stretches that I should do, he got me to run on a treadmill while filming me with his iPad. It was the first time my running had ever been analysed, and I suddenly became very self-conscious and forgot how to coordinate my body properly. I didn't know how fast I should be running either, so kept upping the speed of the treadmill, trying to act like that was my natural running pace.

'Ok, that's enough, you can stop now,' he said.

I slammed my hand on the STOP button and grabbed the handrail tightly as I gasped for breath.

'The problem is...' said the physio, as he re-watched the video of me running. '...and I don't want you to take this the wrong way. But... you don't really look like a runner when you run.'

I wasn't sure how it was possible to interpret this any other way. But, as insulting as it sounded, I completely agreed with him. I don't look like a runner. And it wasn't just because I was feeling self-conscious. Running has never felt natural to me. When you see action shots of decent runners, even in that freeze frame photo, they somehow exude movement. They are often captured with both feet off the ground, floating effortlessly through the air with their arms moving in perfect synchronisation with their legs (although, I saw a behind-the-scenes video of an Instagrammer who showed how these shots are often staged by doing a series of completely unnatural ballet-esque pirouettes as someone snaps away).

Every single photo ever taken of me running has at least one of my feet planted heavily onto the ground and my legs and hip seem to be collapsed to one side with both my arms clenched tightly to my chest.

'No, I don't feel like a runner,' I said, and my heart sank as he showed me the video again.

'I mean, you obviously can run, and you've got a pretty decent level of overall fitness, but because of your style, it is like your body is fighting against itself and making things much more difficult than it should be. That will be part of the cause of your sciatica.'

'What's the solution?'

'Well, there are lots of things we can do to try and improve your running technique. We need to work on your overall mobility. And I would need you to come back for a more thorough analysis.'

This should have been the point at which I booked in several more sessions, but I couldn't really justify paying someone to teach me to run a bit better. I had also been reading a book that claimed that changes to running techniques had little to no effect on overall running performance. Maybe I should just accept that I am an ugly runner.

Looking back after a few more years of discomfort, it would have been money very well spent. Instead, I did nothing about it and used my sciatica as an excuse to cut back on my running significantly.

We spent the May bank holiday weekend at a campsite in Brean, Somerset with Rachel's sister's family. Rachel insisted we hire a static caravan and leave the tent at home.

The caravan was a stone's throw to the beach. But even if you are a stone's throw from a beach along the Bristol Channel, at low tide you might still be what feels like several miles from the sea. At low tide, the sea retreats quickly like bathwater down a plughole, exposing lots of potentially dangerous sinking sand.

The beach at Brean is one of only a handful in the UK that you can legally drive on. This took a while to get used to, with games of cricket being regularly halted while SUVs drove across the wicket, and you would have to look both ways before running to catch a frisbee.

I could see the appeal of on-beach parking, as it made the beach much more accessible to some people, and avoided a long walk carrying all your stuff. Many of the beachgoers then set up camp directly in front of their car. Again, this avoided the need to walk anywhere. At low tide, a beach rescue vehicle patrols the beach, warning beachgoers not to venture too close to the sea because of the sinking sand. And when the tide is out, not only are you not allowed to walk to the sea, but it is so far away you can't even see it. So, you would get the same experience – but with free parking, and no sand in your sandwiches – if you had your picnic in the car park of the local supermarket.

As well as being perfect for beach cricket and beach football (both of which we played a LOT over the course of the weekend), the hard compacted sand was also great to cycle on. We brought four bikes with us to Brean (once again I drew the short straw and there was no room on the car for mine), and the kids made good use of them cycling up and down the beach.

If you have ever driven along the M5 motorway south

Did Not Start

of Bristol, you will probably have noticed Brent Knoll. Brent Knoll is a prominent hill sitting in the middle of the Somerset Levels. At 137 metres, it is not especially high, but it dominates the surrounding area. I had driven by it countless times over the years on journeys to and from Devon. Each time I passed below it while driving back to Northampton to photograph weddings I promised myself I would take the time to stop and walk up it next. But the next time I drove by I was always either in a rush to get to Northampton, or eager to get back to Devon, so talked myself out of the unnecessary detour.

Now that we were staying in Brean for the weekend – just six miles from Brent Knoll – I had no excuse. I enthusiastically mentioned the idea to the rest of the family, but unsurprisingly, walking up a hill was not a tempting alternative to beach cricket or playing in the campsite's amusement arcade. So I was going to have to climb Brent Knoll on my own.

I woke early and borrowed Rachel's bike to cycle the six miles to the village that sits below Brent Knoll, which is imaginatively named Brent Knoll. A dog walker gave me directions to get up the hill, and I followed a road part of the way up by bike and then stuck the bike behind a hedge and continued the rest of the way on foot. The path skirted around a field and then up a fairly steep section of steps towards the top, and before too long I reached the summit. As a National Trust monument, I expected there to be lots of other people making the early morning trip up Brent

Knoll, but I had the entire place to myself.

Brent Knoll was previously known as Mount of Frogs because it was an island haven for wildlife before the surrounding wetlands of the Somerset Levels were drained. Remains of an Iron Age fort are still clearly visible, but it is thought that there has been a human settlement on the hill dating back to before the Bronze Age.

The views were stunning, and I felt an overwhelming sense of peace and wonder. There was a soft haze clinging to the surrounding area below, but this gradually dispersed as I walked the summit's perimeter. Below me, the M5 motorway and the A38 snaked their way through the countryside like they were part of a model village, the gentle hum of traffic just a faint backing track to the early morning birdsong. I never thought the M5 could be considered beautiful, but when viewed from above at first light, it had a strange serenity to it. I wondered whether any of the motorists were looking up at Brent Knoll and making a promise to themselves to one day climb it.

Since my visit to the physiotherapist a couple of weeks previously, I had been sporadically doing my mobility exercises to try and ease my sciatica. I was also trying to focus more on my running style and attempting to run a bit more like a runner. While in Brean, I headed out for my first proper barefoot beach run. It was early evening, but the fog had closed in, reducing visibility to about 20 feet. It was a strange and surreal experience, running along the empty beach, encased in the fog, now with an even greater awareness of my surroundings because of the increased sensation of the cold sand beneath my feet.

My calf muscles and Achilles' tendons felt painful and tight, because of the additional flex they were being put under. I knew this was to be expected when first starting out barefoot running, and it would hopefully ease up over time. But it was a wonderful sensory, childlike experience to be running without shoes, and as cliched as it sounds, it certainly made me feel a closer connection (both literally and metaphorically) to the earth. I wanted more of it.

Every few hundred metres, the wooden posts of the groynes revealed themselves through the fog, stoically doing their bit to attempt to hold back mother nature. Startled flocks of seagulls took to the air at the sight of this strange figure emerging through the haze. *Who was he?* He certainly didn't look like a runner. But he was starting to feel like one. And he had bizarrely started talking about himself in the third person.

NINE

When I completed the River Dart 10k swim, I was certain I would never do it again. I didn't enjoy it and had nothing left to prove. My friends Matt and Charlie loved every bit of the experience and signed up again the following year. I didn't even consider entering and was not in the least bit envious. But I went along to the finish line to cheer them on. My friend Emily (who took part in Ironman Vichy with me) had also come down to Devon to swim the Dart 10k for her first time.

Matt and Charlie emerged from the river, grinning from ear to ear, having somehow enjoyed the swim yet again. Emily emerged soon after with a broad smile too. But hers – like mine – had been a smile of relief that the experience was all over. On previous occasions when spectating at an event – such as Rachel's London Marathon – I have a slight pang of envy that I would prefer to be taking part rather than watching. But standing on the muddy riverbank at the finish line of the Dart 10k, I was very content knowing I had conquered this beast before and didn't have to put myself through it again.

All this changed later that day when I got a text message from Matt and Charlie.

'Good to see you earlier. Thanks for coming along to support. We are signing up for the Dart 10k again next year. Can't wait to get our gold swim hats!'

Swimmers in the Dart 10k are given coloured swim

Did Not Start

hats, depending on their starting group. This is decided by your predicted swim speed. In addition to the different colours, there were a select few who wore a gold swim hat. *Who were these gold-hatted swimmers? What made them so special? Had they paid extra for the privilege? Were they VIPs?*

I had found out from Matt after completing my Dart 10k that gold swim hats are given to those who complete the Dart 10k THREE times.

'*Absolute nutters,*' I had thought to myself. '*Why the hell would anyone swim it THREE times?*'

And now Matt and Charlie were going to be joining this elite band of nutters. Just a couple of ordinary blokes, next year they would each be proud owners of a Dart 10k gold swim hat. I should clarify that these swim hats are identical in every way to the other silicone swim hats. They are just a sort of yellowy-gold colour. But they are still just swim hats.

I replied to Matt and Charlie congratulating them again on their second Dart 10k and telling them I was impressed about their desire to sign up for a third time. I had not been in the least bit bothered about them doing the Dart 10k for a second time, because all they had achieved from that was another yellow swim hat, the same as one I already had from last year. But the gold swim hat? That was a game-changer. I could just picture Matt and Charlie proudly wearing their gold swim hats each time I saw them at the pub or walking around town (not that there was any chance of this ever happening) and that knowing look in their eyes that I had given up after swimming it just the one pathetic time, whereas they had gone on to swim it twice more and had the gold swim hat to prove it.

In that instant, I wanted a gold swim hat more than anything. *Dammit, why hadn't I just signed up like Matt and Charlie this year?* Then next year I too could have been the proud owner of a gold swim hat. But now, in order for me to get my own gold swim hat, I would have to swim it for the next two years, and there would be an entire year of Matt and Charlie lauding it over me for only having done it twice.

But then I had a moment of pure inspiration.

The Dart 10k happens twice each year. Once on the Saturday and once on the Sunday of the same weekend.

What if I signed up for it on both days?

Is that even allowed?

Then I could get my second and third Dart 10ks over and done with, in the same weekend as Matt and Charlie.

And I too could be awarded a gold swim hat.

Author's note

Thank you for choosing to read my book. If you enjoyed it, I would be extremely grateful if you would consider posting a short review on Amazon and help spread the word about my books in any way you can.

You can get in touch via social media:
www.facebook.com/georgemahood
www.instagram.com/georgemahood
www.twitter.com/georgemahood

Or join my mailing list on my useless website to be the first to hear about new releases.
www.georgemahood.com
Signed copies of all of my books are available in my website's 'shop'.

Did Not Finish is a series of books. Please read on…

George Mahood

Book Four...

Did Not Sink – book four in the *DNF* series – is available to order on Amazon.

Here is the blurb...

The lure of a gold-coloured silicon hat is enough to convince George to sign up once again to the Dart 10k swim.
But to get the gold hat, he has to swim it twice.
Despite the trauma of the previous year's Dartmoor Classic, George and Rachel sign up again. This time the weather takes a turn for the worse and Rachel is forced to make some creative wardrobe improvisations.
Having completed several long bike rides, George now considers himself a relatively experienced cyclist.
On the road.
Off-road riding, however, is something completely unfamiliar to him. His body (mostly his more sensitive areas) takes one hell of a beating during his first ever mountain-bike adventure.

Did Not Finish is a series of books about George and his family's adventures in running, cycling and swimming. From ultramarathons to triathlons, 10k swims to European cycling adventures, George promises fun and laughter every step, pedal, and paddle of the way.

BOOK FOUR IN THE DNF SERIES

DID NOT SINK

MISADVENTURES IN RUNNING CYCLING AND SWIMMING

GEORGE MAHOOD

Acknowledgments

First thanks go to all the organisers, marshals and volunteers for putting on these races. Many of them stand outside all day in horrendous conditions, often with no reward or incentive other than the satisfaction of being a part of the event. And perhaps the joy of watching us suffer.

Special thanks to our family and friends who regularly step in to help with childcare while Rachel and I are taking part in these events.

Rachel's editing job for these books was not as scrupulous as usual, which she claimed was because she enjoyed them so much. I think that is only because she features so prominently in them. She would often write 'LOL' in the margin, even though she had been sitting next to me while reading and hadn't made a murmur. Anyway, thank you for lolling (internally).

Becky Beer was as ruthless as ever with the red pen during her proofreading. That's a compliment. Thank you! Please check out her Bookaholic Bex blog (www.bookaholicbex.wordpress.com) and Facebook page.

Thanks to Robin Hommel and Miriam for additional proofreading and feedback.

Thanks to all our friends who have taken part in these challenges and adventures with us. It is always reassuring to not be the only ones with a ridiculously stupid concept of 'fun'.

Did Not Start

Thanks to Rachel… AGAIN (she's even got a starring role in the acknowledgements) for reluctantly agreeing to take part in many of these events with me. We are not always perfect running. cycling, swimming partners, but I wouldn't want it any other way.

Thanks to Layla, Leo and Kitty for putting up with your annoying parents and for continuing to inspire and amuse us. Hopefully one day you will look back and be glad we dragged you out on all these walks.

Thanks to my mum and dad for dragging me out on all those walks when I was younger. I didn't appreciate it at the time, but I do now.

Lastly, thanks to you for reading this series. The idea that people enjoy reading about random things I get up to still feels very bizarre to me, but I'm always honoured and grateful.

Big love.

Also by George Mahood

Free Country: A Penniless Adventure the Length of Britain

Every Day Is a Holiday

Life's a Beach

Operation Ironman: One Man's Four Month Journey from Hospital Bed to Ironman Triathlon

Not Tonight, Josephine: A Road Trip Through Small-Town America

Travels with Rachel: In Search of South America

How Not to Get Married: A no-nonsense guide to weddings… from a photographer who has seen it ALL

(available in paperback, Kindle and audiobook)

Printed in Great Britain
by Amazon